This book is dedicated to our dear friend,
Chef Mohammed Essakhi who first introduced us
to Marrakech and Moroccan cuisine.

Published in Great Britain in 2018 by
Hipmarrakech.com Ltd.
Whiteacres, Cambridge Road, Whetstone,
Leicestershire, LE8 6ZG.
Copyright 2018 Hipmarrakech.com Ltd.

All rights reserved. No part of this publication may be
reproduced or stored in a retrieval system (other than
for the purposes of review) without the express written
permission of the publisher.

A catalogue record for this book is available from
the British Library.

ISBN: 978-1-9993547-0-1

Food photography by Hannah Lansill.
Location photography by Alan Keohane.

Design by Steve Chilton, Chiltz Creative Ltd.

Printed and bound in Great Britain.

MARRAKECH RIAD
COOKBOOK

CONTENTS:

ESSENTIALS..page 9

BREADS & PANCAKES........................ page 19

APPETIZERS, DIPS & SOUPS .... page 31

MAIN COURSES .... page 57

DESSERTS & TEA .... page 81

"If a pot is cooking, the friendship will stay warm."

ARABIC PROVERB

Here at Marrakech Riad we are proud to offer welcoming and authentic Moroccan hospitality. Nowhere is this more evident than in our wholesome and delicious cuisine. Grounded in fresh seasonal produce from the local souks, these magical recipes connect you to an oral tradition that goes back to the foundation of Marrakech a thousand years ago.

These recipes are a selection of the guests' favourites regularly enjoyed in our Riads and taught in our relaxed Cookery School. We invite you to get involved, experiment, and enjoy the flavour of an ancient way of life in your own home with family and friends. Above all, these dishes are meant to be shared. It's fine to divide them into portions and serve on individual plates with cutlery, but why not dine Moroccan-style? Entire families crowd together around the table and eat with their hands from the dish that the food was prepared in.

There is a wonderful flexibility about this cuisine; most dishes are remarkably simple to prepare and readily adaptable. Be confident in the kitchen! There are no rights and wrongs, so feel empowered. Add a little more of a certain spice that you like or swap out one vegetable for another depending on what you have on hand. And most importantly, have fun. Moroccan cuisine is layered, subtle, and exciting, but it should not be daunting. Besaraha! To health and relaxation!

RIAD CINNAMON

ESSENTIALS

PRESERVED LEMON

These salty, citrusy delights are added to many traditional Moroccan dishes. In Morocco, lemons are preserved in two ways: with water and salt, or just with salt. The preserved lemons that are made solely with salt are kept for a very long time—up to four months—and turn dark brown in colour. Darker preserved lemons are used in tangias for both their flavour and their high salt content. To make at home, slice a lemon into eighths (but not all the way through—each slice should still be attached at the bottom) and cover generously in salt. Add to a glass jar with more salt, cover tightly, and store in a dark place until ready to use. For the lighter yellow preserved lemons, follow the same procedure but add a splash of water into the jar before sealing shut. Let the lemons preserve for at least a month before using. We suggest adding these to chicken and fish dishes or your favourite salad dressing. There is no need to rinse the preserved lemons before cooking with them, but remember that because they are so salty you will need to adjust the salt measurements in the rest of the dish accordingly.

RAS AL HANOUT

The name of this spice mix literally translates to "top of the shop" as it is made up of the best spices that each spice shop carries. One of our favorite ras al hanout shops in the medina features cloves, cardamom pods and seeds, nutmeg, cinnamon sticks, star anise, ash and cubeb berries, mace, and ginger root among other ingredients in its mix. We buy it by the kilo (half ground and half whole) right next door to the lovely Henna Cafe on Dar El Bacha.

Ras al hanout can be added to a wide variety of savoury dishes including beef or lamb tagine, couscous, tfaya, or rice with peppers.

SMEN

There are two types of this Moroccan fermented butter: sweet and salty. The salty one has a thick, creamy texture and a very strong, cheesy scent. The other is more waxy in texture and less obtrusive in smell. To make salty smen, boil cow or sheep's milk butter and strain through a cheesecloth before mixing with some salt and/or dried thyme and storing in a khabia a hand-made clay pot specifically made to store smen or khleaa—Moroccan lamb jerky). To make sweet smen, omit the thyme and add in less salt and a bit of sugar to the melted butter. Then, add to a khabia and bury underground for a few months. The longer the butter has to ferment, the more pungent and flavourful it becomes. There are reports that some of the Amazigher peoples buried a khabia of smen when a daughter was born, to be unearthed and enjoyed on the day of her wedding.

ARGAN OIL

Argan oil is referred to as the "liquid gold" of Morocco because it is so rare. The delicate trees it comes from only grow in a very specific microclimate of Morocco: the Sous Valley south and east of Essaouira. The rich cosmetic oil has recently attracted great attention in the beauty industry because it is non-comedogenic and high in antioxidants. Oil is found in the kernel of the argan nut, surrounded by a layer of soft flesh. Many women's cooperatives have sprung up in the Sous Valley region to fulfill the high demand for the precious oil. These cooperatives encourage local women of the region to take part in every aspect of argan oil production and distribution.

To make argan oil for cosmetic use, harvesters wait until the fruits have fallen from the tree before they collect them, dry them out, remove the fleshy part, crack the kernels, and extract their oil. No part of the nut goes to waste; the soft pulp is used as animal feed and the shells are burned for fuel. If the kernels are roasted before being ground, a much darker, rich, nutty oil results. Culinary argan oil (which can help lower cholesterol and ease arthritis) is delicious in salad dressings, drizzled over grilled vegetables, and a must-have when preparing amlou.

PRODUCE

Our food draws on the vegetables, fruits, grains, meats, and fish that are available locally. We prefer to buy directly from growers in the specialist souks that have remained relatively unchanged for generations.

It is worth noting that parsley and coriander are referred to as the "sister ingredients" in the Moroccan kitchen. They are sold together in a mixed bunch, and are referred to as such in these recipes.

DIVERSITY

These dishes and their suggested variants represent an authentic sample of Marrakech Riad cuisine. However, these recipes are not prescriptive. There are endless opportunities for variation in Moroccan cuisine, all of which are equally valid. When you stay with us you will experience that diversity. The cooks in our riad kitchens are encouraged (in fact, they are required) to prepare each dish as they would in their own home while adapting to the seasonal availability of ingredients as well as their personal taste and experience.

Notes:
- In the photograph opposite, cosmetic argan oil is on the left and the darker culinary argan oil is on the right.

GUNPOWDER GREEN TEA

Queen Anne Stuart of Great Britain first gifted Chinese gunpowder green tea to the Sultan of Morocco in the 18th century. The gift was well-received, and the trend of Europeans gifting tea to Morocco continued until eventually the beverage once reserved for the upper class was ubiquitous throughout Morocco. Legend has it that Queen Anne Stuart also presented Moroccans sets of porcelain china to drink from, but they were soon swapped for decorated glass cups. Morocco already had such a surplus of sugar that it was only natural that the tea should be heavily sweetened. Many years ago, Morocco traded Italy sugar for large pieces of marble to use at the El Badi Palace, weight for weight. Herbs began to be added to tea for their medicinal effects, a tradition that still thrives today. Sold in shops and on carts all throughout the Medina, these mint varieties are appreciated for their health benefits as well as for their flavour profiles.

FRESH MINT & HERBS

Spearmint (Na'ana'a) - Gunpowder green tea steeped with spearmint leaves is the national beverage of Morocco: Atay Na'ana'a. Believed to aid digestion, freshen breath, inhibit bacterial growth, and relieve nausea, headaches, and sore throat, this miracle tea is understandably enjoyed throughout the day.

Peppermint (Fliou) - The addition of peppermint leaves to the tea brings about a less sweet, more intense flavour, while also providing the drinker with all of the same health benefits.

Wormwood (Sheeba) - This bitter medicinal herb is thought to treat lack of appetite, anemia, and insomnia. Wormwood is drunk throughout the winter, when its warming effects are especially appreciated.

Lemon Verbena (Louiza) - This tea has a vibrant, bright taste to it. Moroccans drink it because it promotes weight loss, muscle relaxation, anti-inflammation, and provides an immunity boost.

Wild Thyme (Za'atar) - Native to Morocco, this herb is used to season traditional dishes as well (you can find it in smen!). Wild thyme is drunk to relieve joint pain, coughs, colds, or an upset stomach. This is the go-to tea when Moroccans are feeling under the weather.

Sage (Salmia) - This wonderfully aromatic herb is prized for it's calming and warming properties.

Geranium (Atarcha) - The floral, fruity notes of geranium make for a delicious sweet tea with anti-inflammatory qualities.

TAGINE COOKING

The Tagine is a distinctive clay dish with a conical lid. Cooking in a tagine is a unique combination of frying (the tagine is heated from below, traditionally this is done over charcoal); steaming (vapours condense and are collected and recycled down the sides of the lid); and baking (since the whole dish gets hot and radiates a gentle heat in the same way as a chicken brick). The main intervention required is to ensure that there is sufficient moisture as the cooking progresses.

TAGINE ETIQUETTE

Tagine meals are best served straight from the dish. If you are eating Moroccan-style (by hand directly from the pot), you need to understand proper table manners:

First, be sure the tagine is level so the delicious juices don't flow down unfairly to one side. Bread is to be distributed all around, and everyone is encouraged to take as much as they like.

Alternate between dipping the bread into the spiced juices and using it to pick up pieces of vegetable and meat. Gradually work your way in from the outside of the tagine and be sure to only eat from the part that is in front of you. Reaching across to take a tasty piece for yourself is "stealing". If there is a big piece of meat in the centre of the tagine, the tradition is that no one is to touch it until the most senior of the group divides it and shares it out.

If you have an honoured guest—and in Morocco all guests are honoured—you would make a point of taking the juiciest morsel and pushing it across the tagine with great ceremony before insisting that they eat it.

BREADS & PANCAKES

KHOBZ

Makes 4 medium 12 centimetre (5-inch) loaves

Ingredients

250 grams whole wheat (or white) flour
250 grams semolina
1 tablespoon yeast
1 tablespoon sugar
1 tablespoon baking soda
1 teaspoon salt
A bit of olive oil
Barley flour

Method

In a large bowl, whisk the yeast and the sugar into about a cup of warm (not hot) water and let sit for 10 minutes to activate. (If you are using instant yeast you can skip this step.) Add the flour, semolina, baking soda, and salt and mix.

Tip onto a large lightly floured workspace and knead vigorously for 10 minutes. The dough shouldn't be too sticky, if it is add some more flour 1 tablespoon at a time. Let sit for 10 minutes. Divide the dough into four pieces and roll into balls on a lightly floured surface. Let rest for another 10 minutes before flattening gently with your fingertips (again, on a lightly floured surface) to create flat round loaves about 1 centimetre thick.

Brush each loaf with olive oil and cover with barley flour. Lay on a baking sheet or wooden cutting board, cover with a cloth, and carry down the street to the local communal oven. Pay the owner a few dirhams, and come back in an hour or so to retrieve your freshly baked bread.

Notes:

- If you aren't living in Marrakech and don't have access to a communal oven, you can bake your khobz in a 220° C (425° F) oven for 25-30 minutes, or until the bread makes a hollow sound when tapped.
- Khobz is without a doubt the most ubiquitous food item in Morocco. Often referred to as Medina bread, this nutritious whole grain bread is served with every meal. If you eat three times a day, you eat khobz three times a day; if you eat five times a day, you eat khobz five times a day. This bread if always on the table and used in lieu of cutlery. Khobz bread is also used as a form of currency in Marrakech; one piece of khobz is worth one dirham.

MSEMMEN

Makes 15-20

Ingredients

250 grams flour
250 grams semolina
½ tablespoon salt
265 millilitres lukewarm water
Plenty of sunflower oil
A few tablespoons butter

Method

In a large bowl, combine the flour, semolina, and salt. Slowly pour in the water. Knead vigorously for 5 minutes until the mixture resembles a slightly pasty, completely homogenous dough that pulls apart easily. You may find you need to add a few extra tablespoons of flour.

Pour two glugs of sunflower oil onto a dry surface and knead the dough into it for an additional minute to completely cover in oil. Then, cover with cling wrap and let sit for another 10 minutes.

After resting, squeeze the dough through your thumb and forefinger to create golfball sized balls. Set them on an unlined baking sheet to rest, covered in cling wrap, for an additional 5 minutes.

Grab a ball, and flatten it out on a large well-oiled surface with well-oiled hands to create a very thin circular pancake (so thin that you can see through it) about 20 centimetres (8 inches) in diameter. Place about a teaspoon of butter in the middle of the circle and fold the dough into thirds, twice, to create a small square of dough. Don't worry if you get a hole in your msemmen; it's all good.

Meanwhile, heat a cast-iron pan over high heat. After letting the folded dough parcels rest for another 5-10 minutes, gently flatten them out to create large 12 centimetre (5-inch) square pieces, and fry in a generous glug or two of oil until golden brown and slightly crunchy on both sides.

Serve immediately with seasonal jams or mountain honey.

Notes:

- These are eaten up to twice a day in Morocco. Once for breakfast and again in the late afternoon, but always with sweet mint tea.
- Mix pieces of caramelised red onion into the dough before cooking for a savoury Moroccan treat.

AMAZIGH STOVE-TOP BREAD

Makes 2 large loaves or 8 small loaves

Ingredients

375 grams semolina, plus extra for shaping
375 grams flour
2 heaping teaspoons yeast
1 teaspoon salt
265 millilitres warm water

Method

Throw all dry ingredients into a medium-sized bowl. Gradually add the warm water while gently kneading to combine. The dough will naturally form into a ball with a slightly sticky texture. Set aside for 5 minutes to rest.

Remove the dough from the bowl and vigorously knead on a clean surface for 5 minutes. Halve, and then roll each piece into a round ball. Set on an unlined baking sheet to rise until doubled in size (about 30 minutes).

Spread semolina generously over a dry workspace and roll a ball in it until it is completely covered. Then flatten each ball into a disk with your outstretched fingers. If the dough has risen for long enough it will have formed a kind of shell around itself which should easily break from the light pressure of your fingers.

Cook in a very hot cast-iron pan (no oil necessary!), flipping continuously, until slightly browned, about 3-5 minutes. Best served hot with great quality olive oil, mountain honey, argan oil, or amlou (see recipe on page 90).

Notes:
- A delicious substitute to khobz bread, the large loaves pictured here are called Matloa, while the smaller loaves are called Batbout.
- Many families eat this bread in the early hours of the morning before the daily fast begins during the month of Ramadan.
- The Amazigh (Berber) people are indigenous to Marrakech and the Atlas Mountains. They have a proud history and populate an area that extends across North Africa.

BAGHRIR

Makes 15-20 12 centimetre (5-inch) pancakes

Ingredients

125 grams fine semolina
2 tablespoons flour
1 tablespoon sugar
250 millilitres warm water
1 ½ teaspoons baking powder
½ tablespoon of yeast
1 teaspoon salt

Method

This one is super simple: just pop all of the ingredients into a blender and blitz until thoroughly blended. The batter should be runny and frothy—add a bit more water if needed. Ladle small pancakes onto a warm cast-iron pan and cook over medium heat on just one side for 3-5 minutes until golden brown on the bottom and bubbly on top.

Notes:

- These pancakes are traditionally served with a mixture of melted honey and butter, but are equally delicious served with seasonal jams or amlou (see recipe on page 90).

HARSHA

Makes 25-30

Ingredients

235 millilitres sunflower oil
225 grams sugar
110 grams yogurt
4 eggs
4 ½ teaspoons baking powder
1 ½ tablespoons vanilla sugar (or substitute a few drops of vanilla extract)
1 ¼ teaspoons salt
The juice of one large orange
850 grams semolina

Method

Mix the first eight ingredients together in a large bowl and slowly add in the semolina until the mixture is sticky but moves from one side of the bowl to the other easily when turned. You may end up using more or less than 835 grams of semolina.

To shape each harsha, remove a small fistful of the dough and flatten between your palms. Use your thumbs to mold into the size of a saucer about 1 centimetre thick and cover in semolina.

Set the harsha aside for 10 minutes and then cook them in a cast-iron pan over medium high heat until browned on either side (about 5 minutes total). You don't need to butter or oil the pan before cooking, although you can if you would like. We recommend you use a spatula to make this process much easier, as the harsha are quite fragile before being cooked. Serve warm drizzled with mountain honey.

Notes:
· Sunflower oil is often replaced by an equivalent quantity of butter.
· Make savoury harsha by stuffing before cooking with meat, cheese, or vegetables.
· These freeze well! Simply warm up again on a hot frying pan before serving.

RIAD STAR

APPETIZERS, DIPS & SOUPS

ZAALOUK

Serves 2

Ingredients

3 aubergines
2 tomatoes
35 grams tomato paste
2 teaspoons black pepper
2 teaspoons ground ginger
2 teaspoons paprika
2 cloves garlic
Salt, to taste
Vegetable oil, for frying
Chopped fresh parsley and coriander, to garnish

Method

Chop the aubergines (eggplants) up into 1 centimetre cubes (no need to peel beforehand!) and fry in plenty of vegetable oil, stirring occasionally, until golden brown in colour (about 10 minutes). To ensure even cooking, feel free to work in batches so as not to overcrowd the pan. Remove from oil and let drain on a paper towel.

Meanwhile, halve the tomatoes horizontally and grate with a box grater to create a pulpy juice. The skin will naturally come off as you do this. Discard the skin.

Heat the tomato pulp in a cast-iron pan. Add the tomato paste, spices, and a glug of vegetable oil. Reduce heat to low and stir to combine. Simmer, stirring occasionally. Meanwhile, mince the garlic, and throw it in. Let cook for another 2 minutes. Add the aubergines and stir to combine, using a fork to smash everything together. Serve warm or cold, garnished with parsley and coriander.

Notes:

· Add a bay leaf to the oil or turmeric to the sauce for a different flavour, if you prefer.

TAKTOUKA

Serves 4

Ingredients

3 tomatoes
3 cloves garlic
3 bell peppers (we use red, green, and yellow)
A generous glug of olive oil
1 teaspoon paprika
1 teaspoon turmeric
A handful of chopped fresh parsley and coriander
Salt and pepper, to taste

Method

Halve the tomatoes, mince the garlic, and slice the peppers. Grate the tomato halves over a saucepan and discard the skin that will naturally peel off. Warm the resulting tomato pulp over medium heat and then pour in a generous glug of olive oil. Plop in the peppers, garlic, spices, and parsley and coriander. Sauté for 15-20 minutes and serve warm. It's as easy as that!

Notes:

· Add a bay leaf, ground ginger, or cumin for different flavour. Or, add a splash of white vinegar to the taktouka just before you take it off of the heat and serve.

PUMPKIN SALAD

Serves 4

Ingredients

250 grams of pumpkin
4 teaspoons vanilla sugar (or substitute a few drops of vanilla extract)
1 tablespoon of sugar
1 teaspoon cinnamon
A few drops of orange flower water
A handful of golden raisins

Method

Remove the skin and seeds from the pumpkin (or squash), cut in half and then into thirds, and boil in enough water to cover until tender. Drain. Plop into a pan with the other ingredients and cook altogether, mashing with a fork, for 5 minutes. Serve warm topped with a sprinkling of cinnamon.

Notes:

· Substitute parsnips or carrots for pumpkin and add a dash of cream while cooking.

MOROCCAN TOMATO SALAD

Serves 4

Ingredients

3 tomatoes
½ a red onion
A handful of chopped fresh parsley and coriander
Good quality olive oil
Salt and pepper, to taste

Method

Peel the red onion and remove the seeds and skin from the tomatoes, then finely dice both. Throw into a bowl with the parsley and coriander, a good drizzle of olive oil, and salt and pepper to taste.

Notes:

- Be sure to use good quality olive oil here.
- This salad is open to interpretation. Try adding diced avocado, cucumber, bell pepper, a bit of white vinegar, or a squeeze of lemon juice.
- This is sometimes referred to as the Moroccan National Salad, perhaps because red and green are the colours of the Moroccan flag.

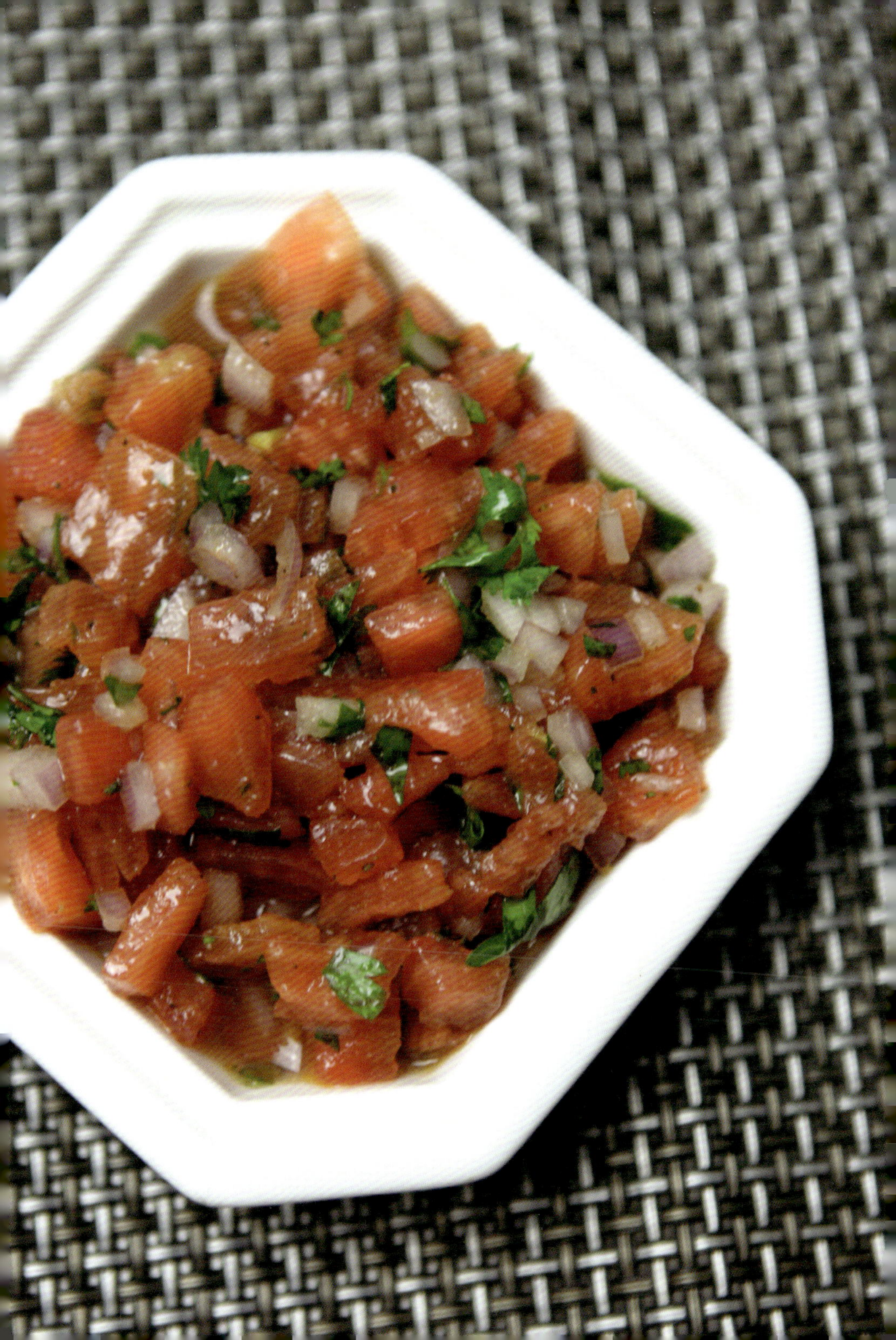

COURGETTE SALAD

Serves 4

Ingredients

5 small courgettes
4 garlic cloves
A small handful of chopped fresh parsley and coriander
1 tablespoon olive oil
1 teaspoon turmeric
½ teaspoon ground ginger
Salt and pepper, to taste

Method

Coarsely grate the courgettes (zucchini) over a medium saucepan. Rotate each courgette as you grate, and discard the resulting white cores. Mince the garlic and add it in with the parsley and coriander, spices, and olive oil. Sauté over high heat for about 5 minutes. Add a splash of water to the pan, and continue to sauté for another 5 minutes. Serve warm.

Notes:

- For another courgette salad, thinly slice the courgettes into circles. Fry with about a tablespoon of butter, a sprinkle of white vinegar, some lemon juice, and chopped fresh parsley and coriander. Add salt and pepper to taste.

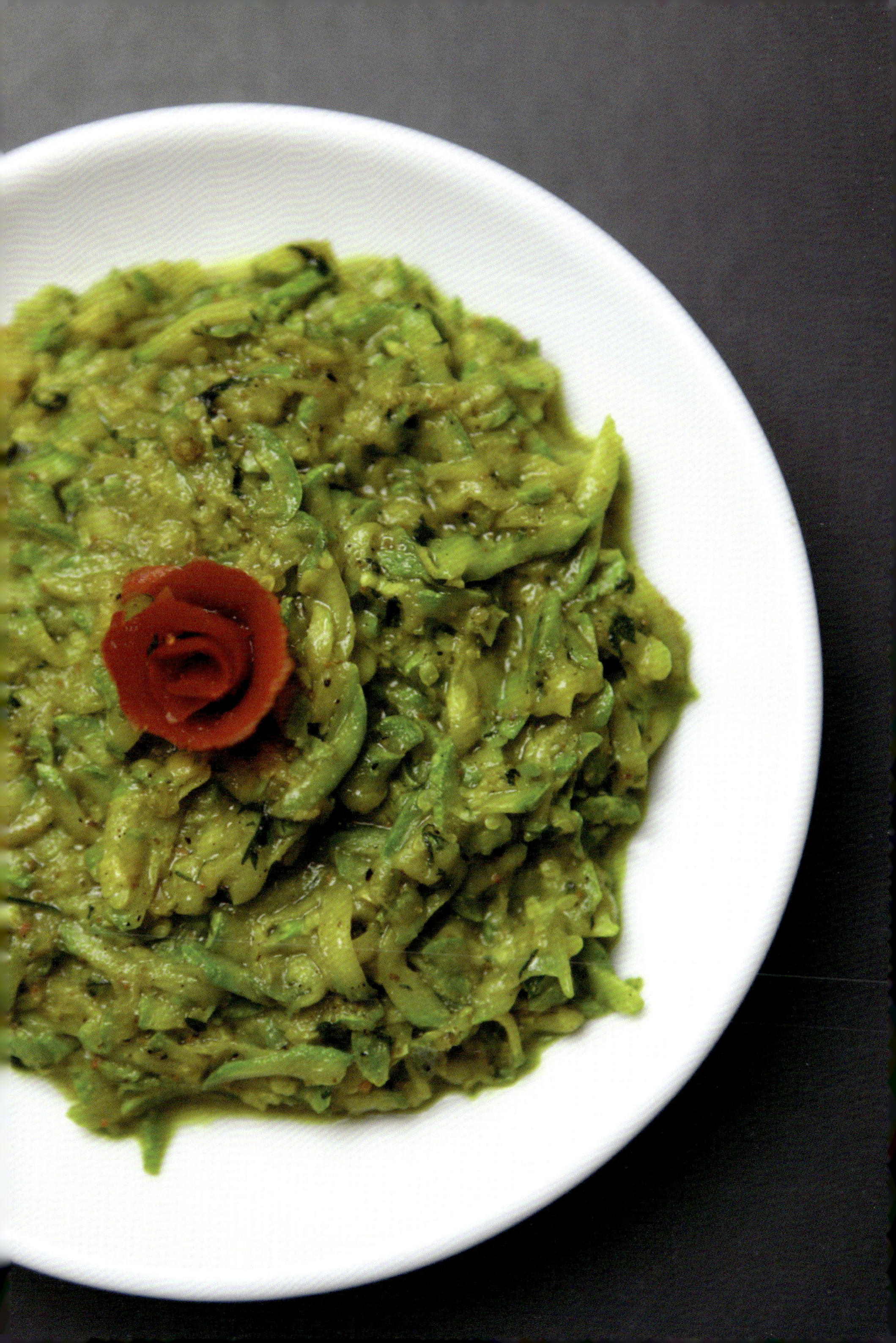

BEET SALAD

Serves 4

Ingredients

3 medium beets
½ a red onion
A splash of white vinegar
Chopped fresh parsley and coriander
A sprinkle of cumin
Salt and pepper, to taste

Method

Boil beets in a saucepan until you can easily cut through them with a knife, about 20-25 minutes. Meanwhile, very finely dice the red onion. Drain the beets and immediately place them in a bowl of cold water to stop the cooking process. Peel off the skin and roughly dice. Add to a bowl with the rest of the ingredients and stir to combine. Taste, and add some more cumin if needed. Serve chilled.

Notes:

- Another wonderful beet salad is made by boiling beets and then mixing with a few tablespoons of plain yogurt (about 110 grams) and a handful of chopped fresh parsley and coriander.

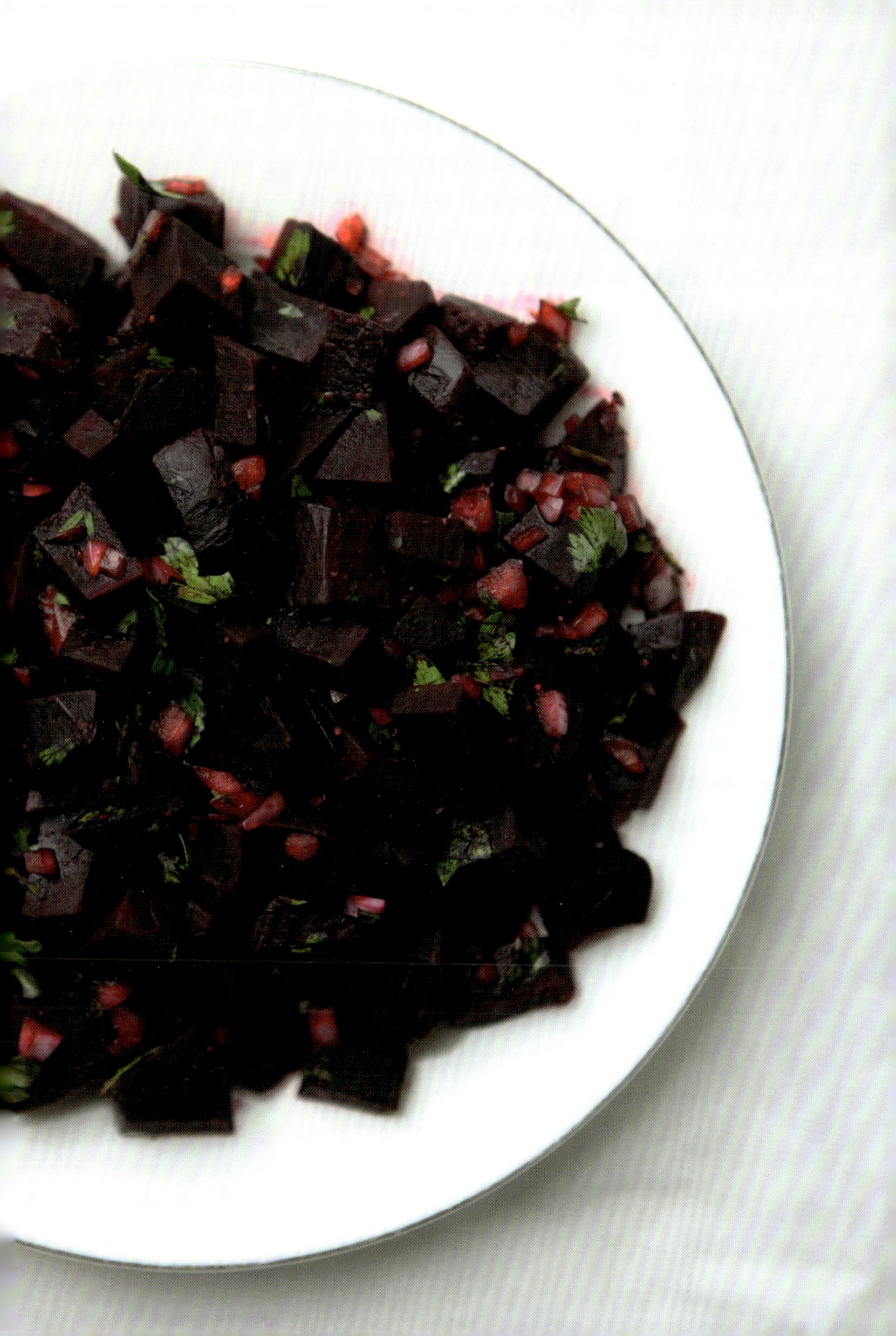

RICE WITH PEPPERS

Serves 4

Ingredients

360 grams rice
3 bell peppers (we use red, green and yellow)
A generous glug of olive oil
A small handful of chopped fresh parsley and coriander
Salt and pepper, to taste

Method

Deseed and finely dice the peppers, and then cook in a cast-iron pan with oil. Add salt and pepper to taste. Sauté for 10 minutes, stirring often to prevent burning. Meanwhile, cook the rice. When ready, add the cooked rice to the pan and stir to combine. Serve warm sprinkled with parsley and coriander.

Notes:

- We love swapping peppers for carrots, peas, corn, or mushrooms but you can get as creative as you'd like!
- You can add 1 ½ teaspoons paprika, turmeric, ground ginger, or ras al hanout to this recipe for more intense flavour.
- You can swap out the olive oil for butter for a creamier dish.

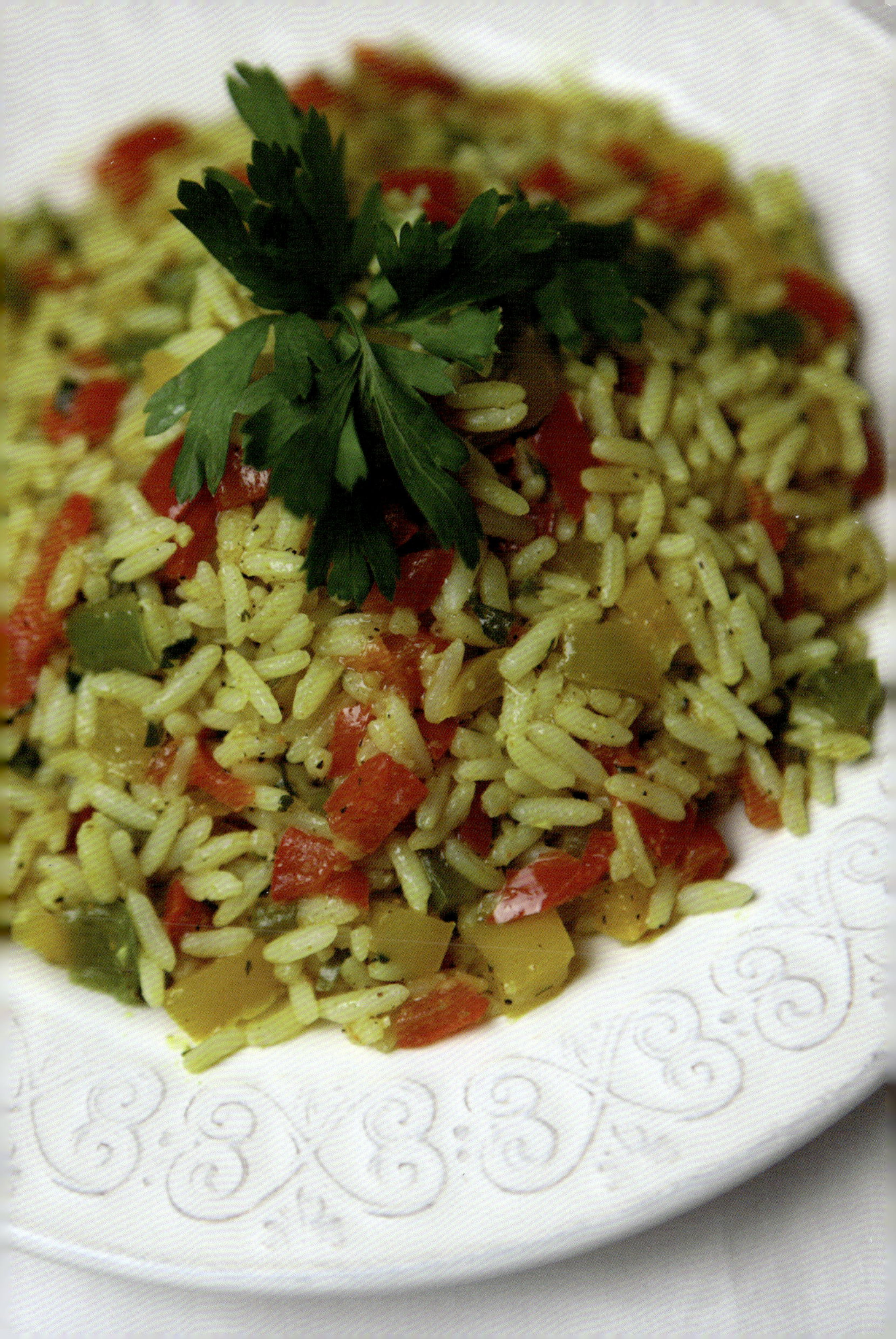

BRIOUATES

Serves 4

Ingredients

1 chicken breast
2 small courgettes
1 medium carrot
3 cloves garlic
5 saffron threads
30 grams sliced green olives
1 teaspoon paprika
½ teaspoon turmeric
½ teaspoon ground ginger
Salt and pepper, to taste
A small handful chopped fresh parsley and coriander
90 grams goat cheese
A few sheets of filo pastry
Olive Oil
1 egg

Method

Mince the garlic, and add to a large saucepan with a glug of olive oil. Warm over medium high heat for 1 minute, or until fragrant. Finely dice the chicken and cook until browned on all sides, stirring frequently, for approximately 7 minutes. Grate the courgette and carrots and add in with the saffron and olives. Stir to combine. Add the spices and 30 millilitres water. Cook for another 5 minutes over medium heat, then add the parsley and coriander. Remove from heat and set aside.

Peel apart a layer of filo dough and lay out flat. Cut into large strips about 7 centimetres (2 ½ inches) in width. Place a heaped spoonful of the chicken mixture and a bit of cheese on one end of the filo dough strip. Roll the briouate from right to left, then left to right, to create a triangularly shaped parcel. Beat the egg and brush over the briouate to seal it shut and then place on an unlined baking sheet. Bake at 200°C (390°F) for 10-15 minutes or until golden brown. Brush with melted butter and return to oven for another 10 minutes. Serve immediately.

Notes:

- Traditionally, Moroccans eat briouates stuffed with homemade goat cheese called jebli, but any melting cheese will do. Edam is particularly popular in Marrakech, but you can try these out with gouda, fontina, or cheddar, too.

- You can fill your briouates with just about anything. Try these with kefta (remove the veggies, olives, and saffron and throw in some cumin instead), ground beef (ditto, and throw in some ras al hanout as well), fish or shrimp (you can just swap it in for the chicken). For a sweeter almond briouate, grind roasted shelled almonds together with some sugar, then knead in cinnamon, a dash or two of orange flower water, and a pinch of salt for the filling. After the briouates are cooked, soak in warm honey for 3-5 minutes. Strain and let cool before serving.

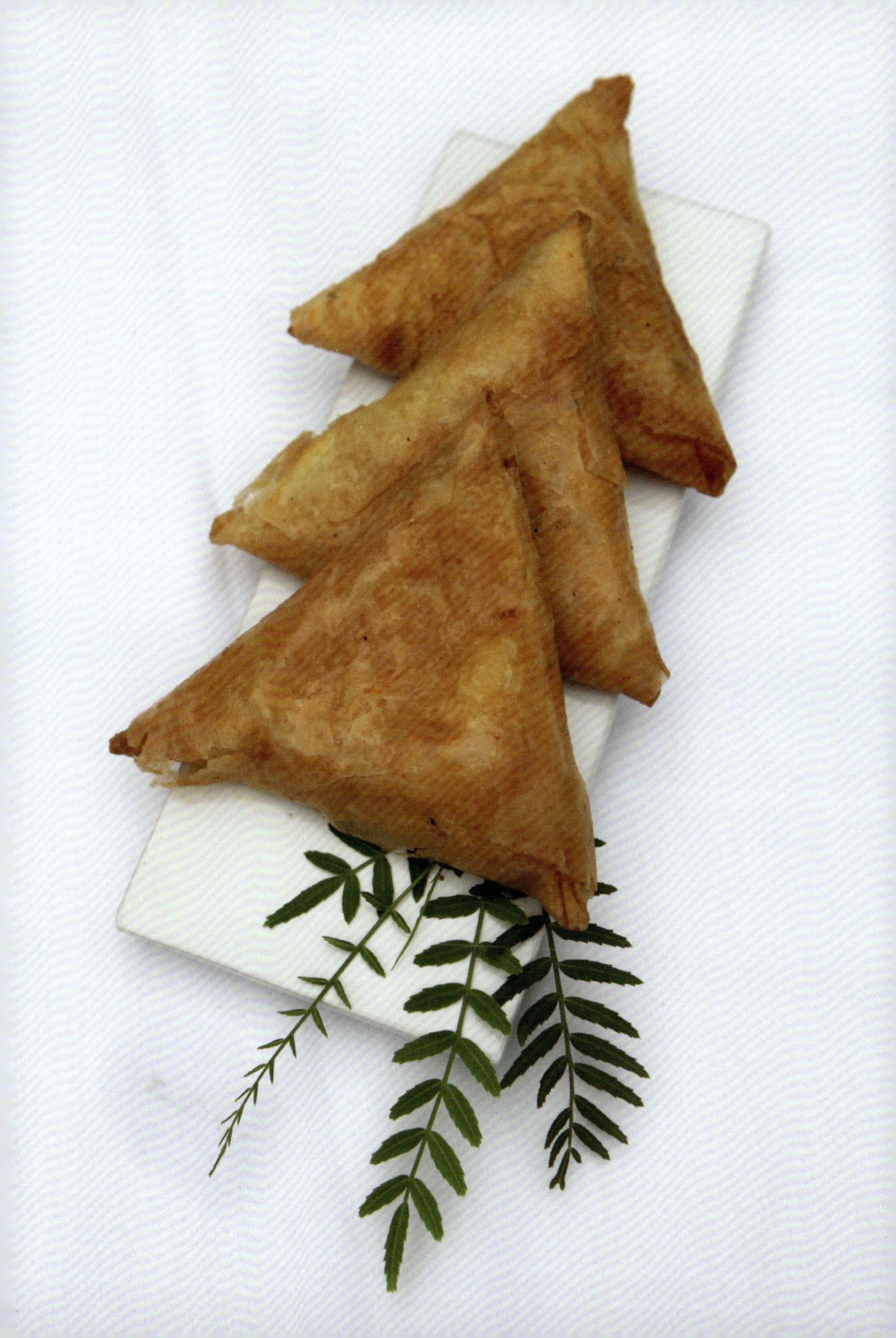

FRIED CAULIFLOWER

Serves 2

Ingredients

½ a head cauliflower
2 eggs
A small handful of chopped fresh parsley and coriander
Salt and pepper, to taste
Sunflower oil, for frying

Method

Trim the leaves from the cauliflower and then cut into large pieces. In a small bowl, beat the eggs with parsley, coriander, salt, and pepper. Dip the cauliflower into the egg mixture until thoroughly covered. Pour a generous amount of sunflower oil into a pan and—only once it's very hot—add the cauliflower. Fry on each side until browned, about 15 minutes total. Remove from heat and set on a paper towel to sop up any excess oil. Best served warm sprinkled with additional parsley and coriander.

Notes:

· Try this with courgette, carrots, or sweet potato as a Moroccan twist on tempura.

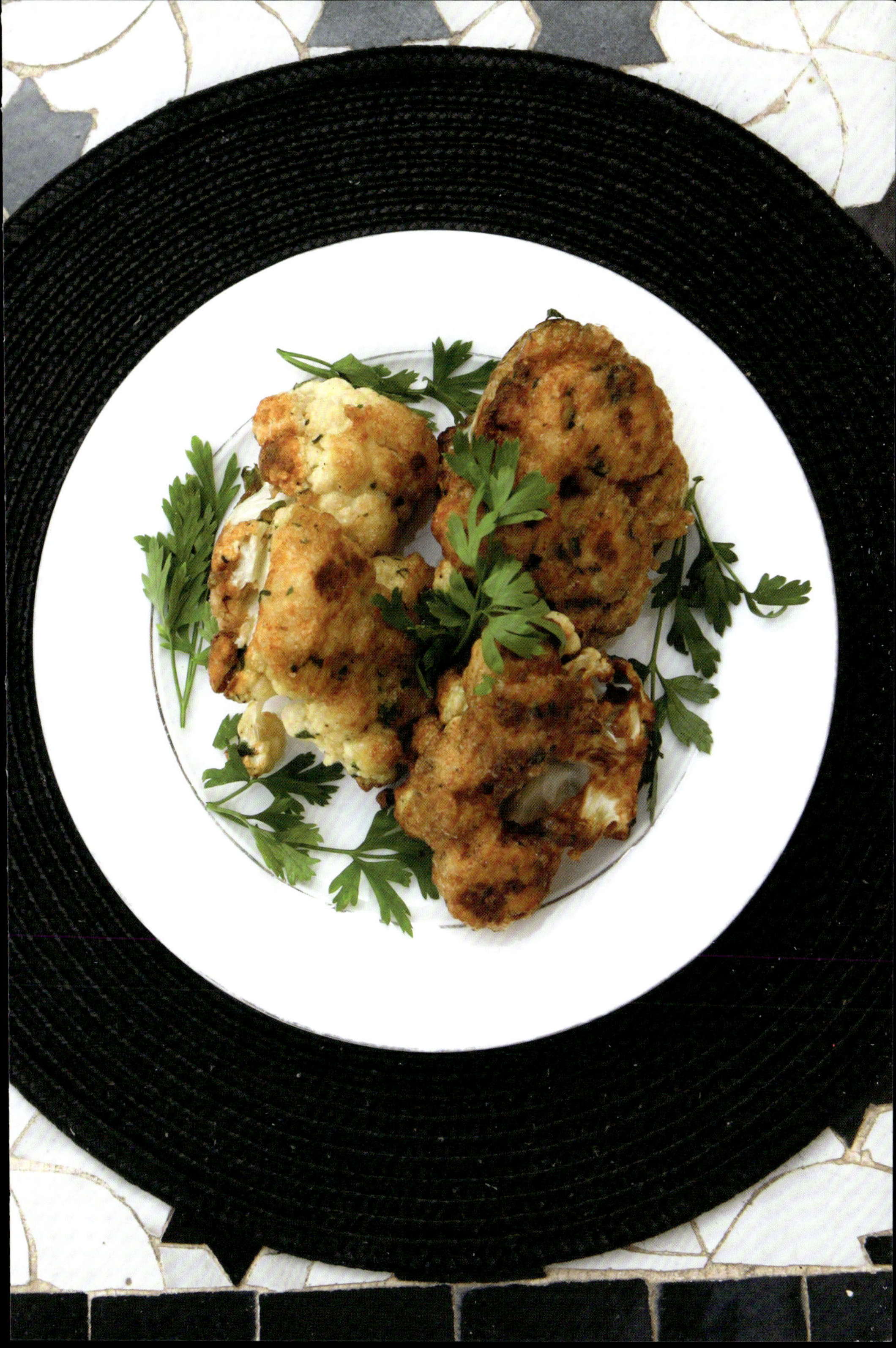

MAAKOUDA

Serves 4

Ingredients

500 grams potatoes
A knob of smen (or ghee, or any other clarified butter)
A small handful of chopped fresh parsley and coriander
Salt and pepper, to taste
1 egg
60 grams raclette cheese (or any other melting cheese)
1 tablespoon corn flour
Vegetable oil, for frying

Method

Peel and cut potatoes into large pieces. Boil with a teaspoon of salt until they are tender, about 20 minutes. Drain. Return to the pot with the smen, parsley, and coriander. Mash together with a hand masher. Crack in the egg, grate in the cheese, and throw the corn flour in, too. Mix until very well combined.

Using two spoons, shape the potato dough into oblong balls (in French cuisine, this is called a quenelle). Drop into very hot vegetable oil and cook until golden brown. Set on a paper towel to remove any excess oil and serve immediately.

Notes:

· Best cooked in a cast-iron frying pan.

· Make sure the oil is very hot before cooking, or else the maakouda will fall apart.

· Try these with aioli or fresh mayonnaise.

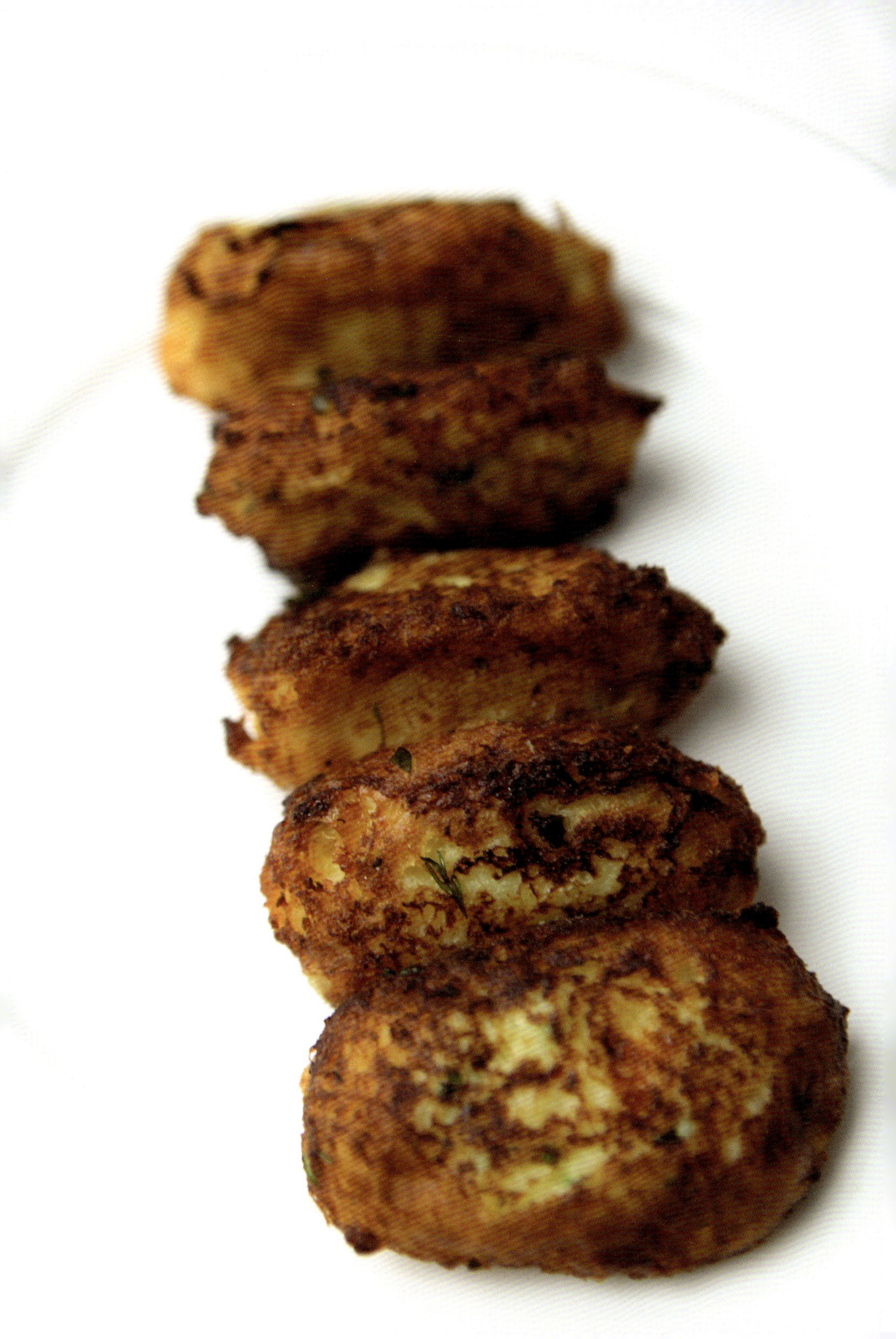

BESSARA

Serves 4

Ingredients

250 grams dried green peas (or use green split peas)
4 cloves garlic
About 125 millilitres of good quality olive oil
1 ½ teaspoons cumin
Paprika
Salt, to taste

Method

Put the peas in a bowl and pour in enough water to just cover, then let 'em soak overnight. Drain, skin (if they haven't been already), rinse well, and toss into a pot. Peel the garlic cloves and add to the pot with the olive oil, a teaspoon of cumin, and the paprika. Pour in cold water until the peas are covered, top with a lid, and cook until the peas are splitting apart (about an hour). Turn off the flame, and let the bessara cool a bit before tipping into a blender and blitzing until smooth. Pour back into the pot, and grab a small glassful of water. Mix in another pinch of paprika and ½ a teaspoon of cumin, and pour the spiced water into the soup. If you'd like a thinner soup, feel free to add more water. Stir and cook for another 3-5 minutes. Ladle the bessara into bowls and top with olive oil, a sprinkle of cumin, and salt to taste. Serve warm with khobz.

Notes:

- Bessara is a traditional Moroccan winter soup. However, by simply adding less water while cooking, this recipe makes for a delicious dip to be eaten during the warmer months. Serve warm or chilled topped with smoked paprika, lemon juice, salt, and olive oil. Dip in a variety of sliced veggies, bread, or pita chips.
- Fava beans can be substituted for peas, or used in combination. No matter how you prepare this dish, be sure to use good quality olive oil as its rich, almost spicy flavour will really stand out.

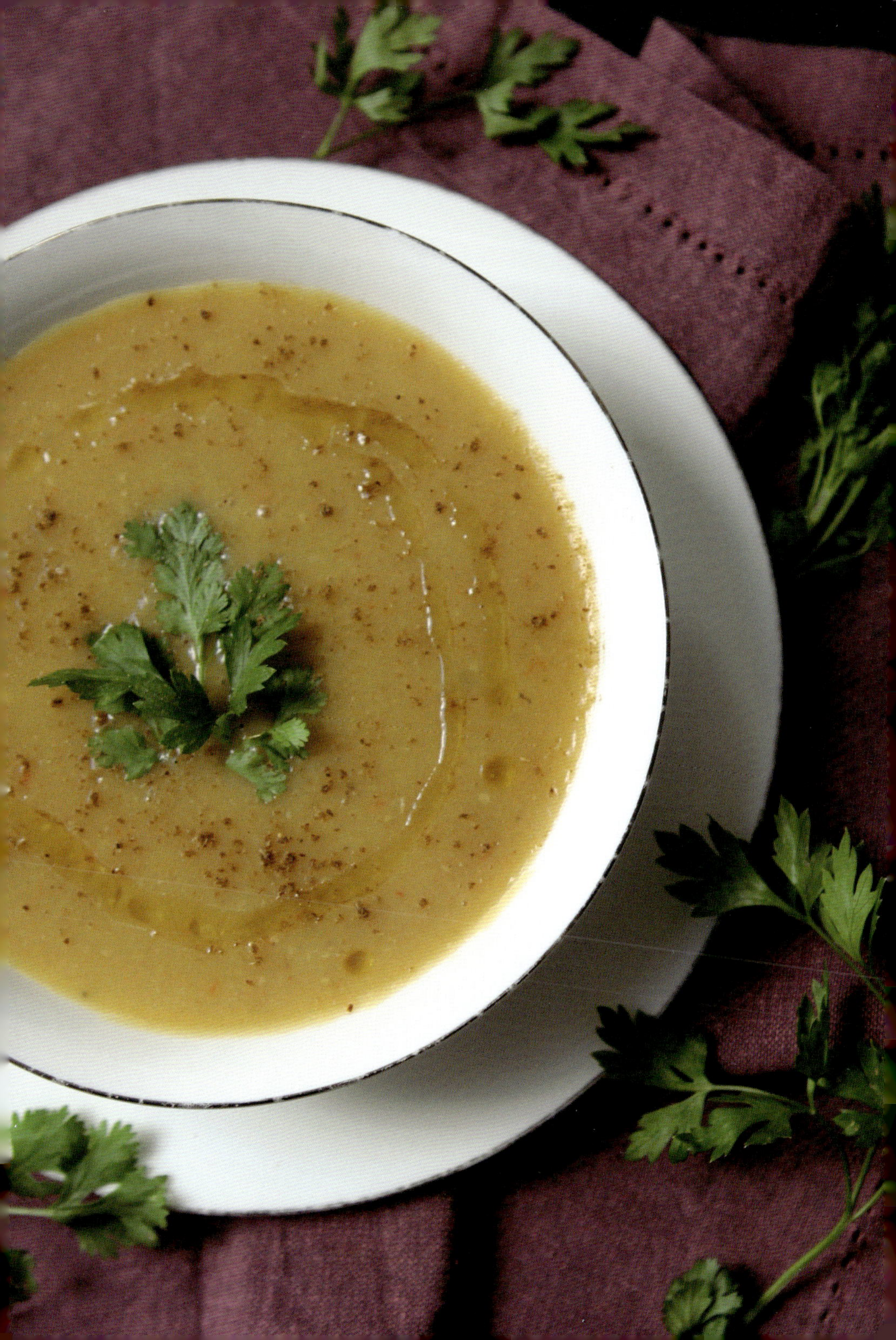

HARIRA

Serves 5

Ingredients

100 grams dried chickpeas
100 grams dried broad beans
100 grams dried green lentils
100 grams uncooked rice
60 millilitres olive oil
50 grams vermicelli
2 tablespoons flour
2 tomatoes, quartered
1 small red onion, quartered

1 ½ tablespoons tomato paste
1 tablespoon smen (or ghee, or any other clarified butter)
1 beef stock cube (or make your own beef stock from beef bones and use 500 millilitres)
¾ teaspoon each: turmeric, paprika, ground ginger, cinnamon
A large bunch of parsley and coriander
Salt and pepper, to taste

Method

In a blender, blitz half of the parsley and coriander with the red onion, tomatoes, and 750 millilitres of water until very finely blended. Add to a very large pot with chickpeas, broad beans (fava beans), and lentils. Cook altogether over high heat for 20 minutes, then add the spices, beef stock (cubed or homemade) and olive oil. Cover and cook over high heat for half an hour.

Meanwhile, rinse out the blender and then throw in the tomato paste, flour, and 500 millilitres of water. Blitz until combined. Set aside.

Uncover the soup pot, and add the rice and another 600 millilitres of water. Continue cooking over high heat for another 15 minutes before adding vermicelli. Cook for another 30 minutes, then add the tomato paste/flour/water mixture while stirring.

Chop the remaining parsley and coriander, and toss in with salt and pepper to taste. Throw in the smen, and give the harira a good stir. Serve warm.

Extras (use one or all):

- Roasted shredded chicken breast
- Roast beef, cut into bite-size pieces
- Egg (After adding the tomato paste/flour/water mixture, whisk an egg in a bowl and pour into the soup slowly as you use your other hand to stir. Let it bubble for a minute or two to let the egg cook through.)

Notes:

- This hearty, comforting soup is traditionally served as a central part of the breakfast meal during the holy month of Ramadan. It is normally accompanied by dates and shebbakiya (a sticky honey and sesame cookie). Rustic wooden spoons are synonymous with harira; these are hand crafted in the Atlas Mountains near Marrakech.
- If it is difficult to find dried broad beans in your local grocery store, you can use canned or frozen. Or, substitute in lima beans, butterbeans, or another pulse.

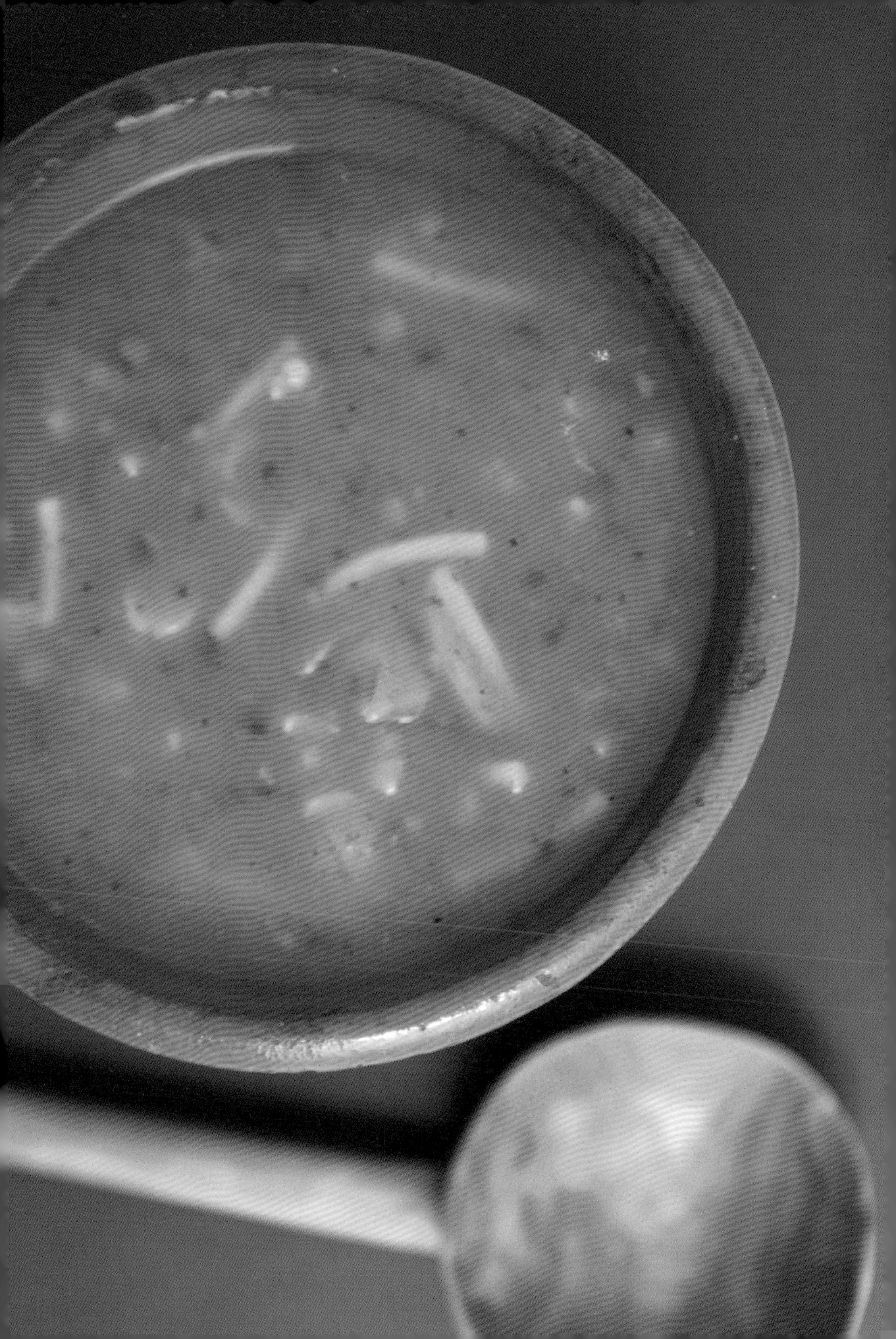

DAR HABIBA

MAIN COURSES

CHICKEN PASTILLA

Serves 4

Ingredients

For the chicken:

1 whole chicken (approximately 1 ½ kilos)

The juice of 2 lemons

A large handful of chopped fresh parsley and coriander

2 cloves garlic, finely chopped

1 tablespoon ras al hanout

1 teaspoon ground ginger

1 teaspoon turmeric

Just a pinch of freshly ground nutmeg

3 tablespoons olive oil

1 red onion, diced

Salt and pepper, to taste

For the eggs:

4 eggs

For the almonds:

150 grams raw almonds

2 tablespoons sunflower oil

4 tablespoons sugar

1 tablespoon cinnamon

To assemble:

4 large circular sheets of filo pastry (or cut rectangular sheets into circles if needed)

1 egg

1 tablespoon butter

To top:

Powdered sugar

Cinnamon

Method

Rub the chicken with lemon juice and plenty of salt. Remove any fat, then rinse under running water before placing in a pot with the rest of the ingredients and 100 millilitres of water. Cover and cook over medium high heat for 1 hour.

Meanwhile, blanch the almonds and then fry in sunflower oil until golden brown. Strain out any excess oil and then toss into a grinder with sugar and cinnamon. Blitz until very finely ground. Set aside.

Once the chicken is cooked through, remove from the pot and set on a plate to cool. Turn the heat up under the remaining sauce until bubbling and drop in 4 eggs. Whisk and stir until the mixture resembles a soft scramble. Set aside.

Once the chicken has cooled for 10-15 minutes, remove the bones and shred finely.

To assemble the pastilla, lay out 2 sheets of filo pastry flat on a large workspace. Place the chicken mixture in the middle and flatten until about 2 centimetres thick. Be sure to leave about 5 centimetres of uncovered filo dough around the edges. Then layer on the egg mixture, flattening to about 1 centimetre thick, and finally the almond mixture which will be about half a centimetre thick.

Crack an egg into a bowl and whisk. This is your adhesive. Fold the uncovered edges of filo dough up and on top of the filling. Then brush the visible part of the filo dough with egg wash. Top with 2 more sheets of filo dough, and fold them underneath the pastilla to seal in the filling. Brush egg wash all over the top of the pastilla, and then brush with melted butter. Bake in a preheated 180° C (350° F) oven for 45 minutes, or until golden brown.

Top with powdered sugar and cinnamon. Serve.

Notes:
- This crowd-pleasing dish is traditionally made for special occasions with pigeon meat.
- For a vegetarian pastilla, use 1 ½ kilos grated mixed vegetables and vermicelli in place of the chicken and follow the recipe as normal.
- For a seafood pastilla, sauté ½ a kilo each of shelled shrimp and cubed white fish with 2 bay leaves, a teaspoon each cumin, paprika and salt, 1/2 a teaspoon ground ginger, 2 minced garlic cloves, some olive oil, chopped fresh parsley and coriander, and a handful of dried black mushrooms in a pot over medium high heat. Boil 1/2 a kilo prawns separately and then shell before adding in with the rest of the seafood. Once combined, add 1 tablespoon of tomato paste and a cup of water. In a separate bowl, soak a large handful of vermicelli in warm water for 5 minutes to soften. Drain, cut to desired length, and add in with the seafood. Squeeze a lemon on top and throw in a bit of harissa if you want some spice. Once cooked through, remove the bay leaves and cool. Assemble the pastilla as stated above. Bake until golden brown and then top with shredded edam cheese once out of the oven. Serve immediately.

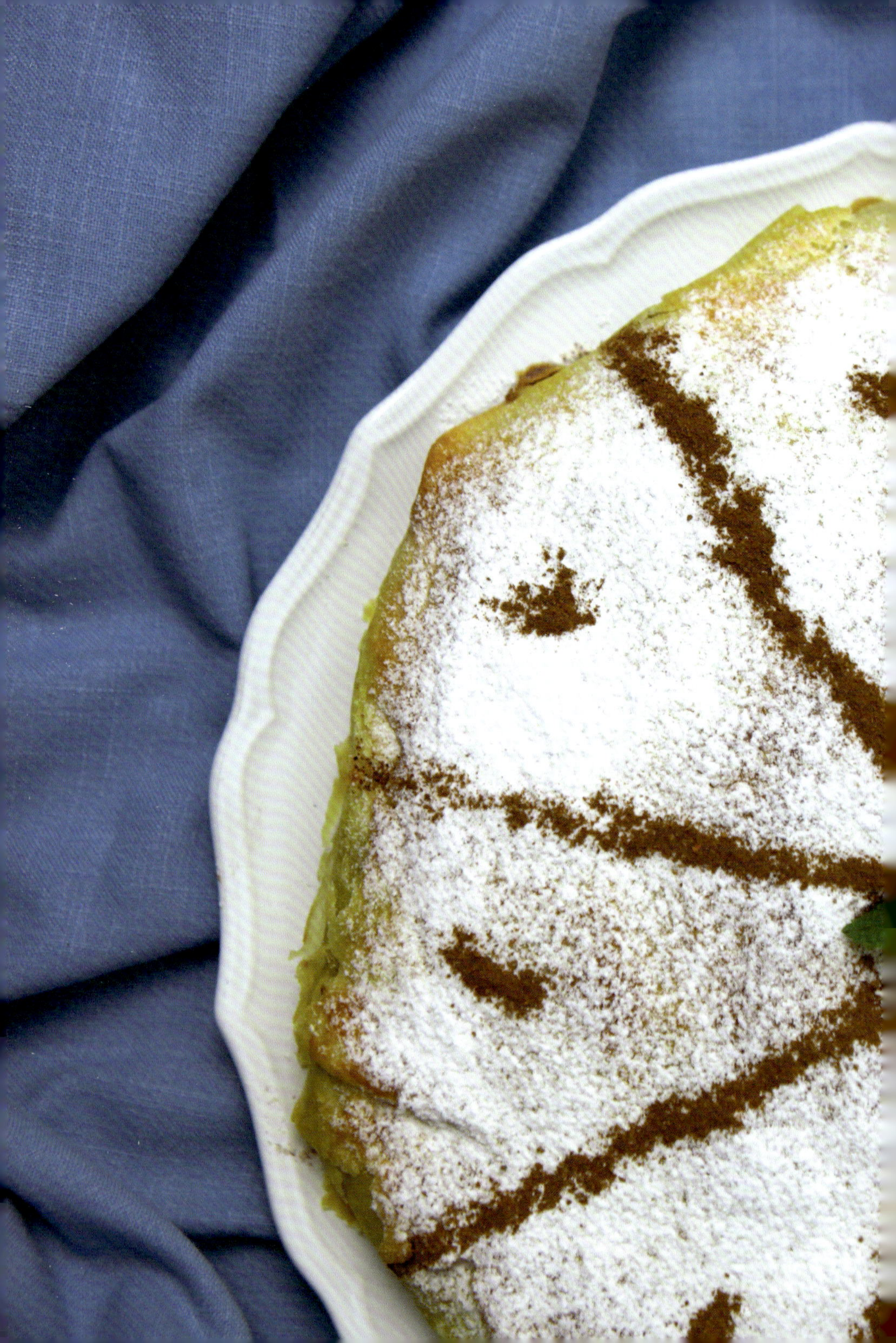

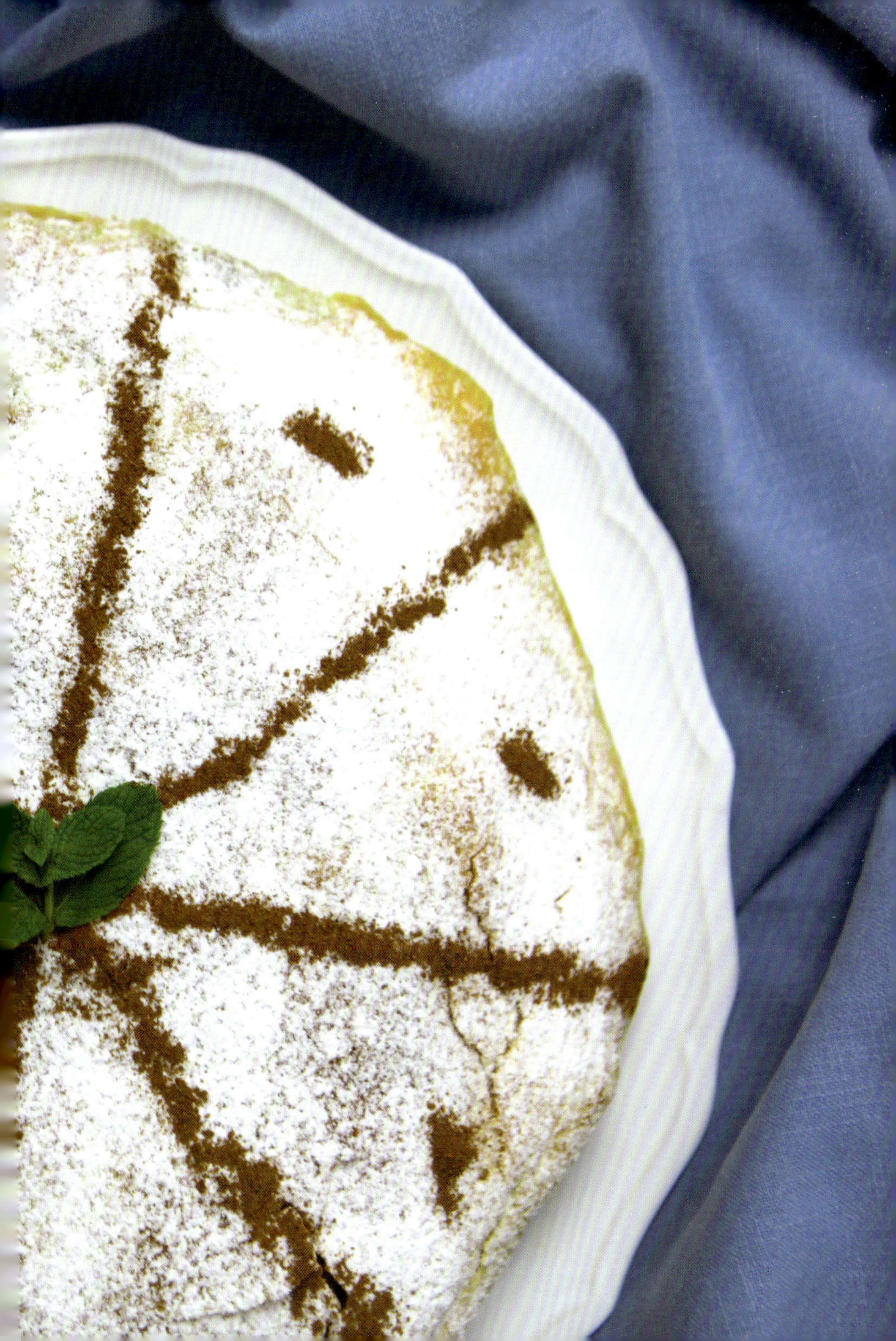

COUSCOUS ROYALE

Serves 15

Ingredients

1 kilo couscous

2 red onions

1 kilo mixed vegetables: tomato, carrot, aubergine, turnip, courgette, cabbage, pumpkin

200 grams chickpeas

½ kilo lamb, cut into 1-inch cubes

½ kilo beef sausages

½ kilo chicken drumsticks

1 tablespoon of smen (or ghee, or any other clarified butter)

1 tablespoon tomato paste

One small bunch of fresh parsley and coriander

4 teaspoons ground ginger

4 teaspoons turmeric

4 teaspoons paprika

1 teaspoon ground saffron

Olive oil

Salt and pepper, to taste

Method

Halve one of the red onions and then thinly slice before tossing into a couscoussier. Set aside a few sprigs of parsley and coriander before using a string to tie a knot around the rest of the small bunch and throw that in, too. Skin the tomatoes and dice them, then add to the couscoussier along with 2 glugs of olive oil and a generous teaspoon of each spice. Stir and let cook for 10 minutes over low heat to avoid burning the red onions.

Add 2 ½ litres of water to the couscoussier and turn the heat all the way up. Meanwhile, prepare your vegetables: peel and halve the carrots and turnips, trim and halve the aubergines, and quarter the cabbage. Add everything to the couscoussier with the chickpeas. Top with the top half of the couscoussier and cook for an hour.

Meanwhile, add the couscous to a large flat round bowl and splash with about 225 millilitres of cold water. Pour the water onto your hand over the couscous so that it splashes all around, then mix to combine. Add the couscous to the top part of the couscoussier (or double boiler with holes on the bottom) and cook until it starts steaming. After the vegetables beneath have cooked for an hour, remove the top part of the couscoussier and add in the pumpkin, courgette, and tomato paste. Once the couscous starts steaming, place back into the flat round bowl and splash with another 225 millilitres of cold water. Let it cool for a minute before splashing with 3 glugs of olive oil. Rub the couscous together with your hands until well-combined and then return to the top of the couscoussier.

Check on the vegetables and add another 1 ½ litres or so of water if necessary. Once the couscous starts steaming again, remove it and add in 225 millilitres of water and

1 teaspoon of salt. Mix together with your hands and then return to the top of the couscoussier. Once it starts steaming again, mix in the smen and another 300 millilitres of water. Return to the top of the couscoussier and cook until it starts steaming once again.

About halfway through this process, grab three bowls and place each meat in a bowl. Mince the second red onion and add a third to each bowl along with 1 teaspoon each of paprika, ground ginger, turmeric, salt, pepper, and a generous sprinkling of chopped fresh parsley and coriander (remember the sprigs you set aside earlier?). Mince 3 cloves of garlic and throw 1 into each bowl as well. Let marinate for half an hour and then cook in three separate pots with a bit of olive oil. Add in a few splashes of water while cooking to ensure the meat is moist. Note that the chicken will cook more quickly than the other meats.

Pile the cooked lamb meat in the middle of a large flat round bowl and then top with the finished couscous. Top with tfaya and then arrange the chicken and sausages around the sides. Using a slotted spoon, remove the vegetables and arrange them around the couscous as well. Spoon the delicious sauce from the vegetables into a bowl and serve alongside the couscous.

Notes:

- If you are using dry chickpeas, be sure to soak them overnight beforehand.
- Couscous is eaten on Fridays, and the whole family makes great efforts to be together to eat the large, time-consuming dish.

TFAYA

2 large red onions
2 cinnamon sticks
1 teaspoon pepper
½ teaspoon cinnamon
⅛ teaspoon ground ras al hanout
⅛ teaspoon ground saffron
⅛ teaspoon ground turmeric
A splash of olive oil
1 tablespoon sugar
A handful of golden raisins

Method

Very thinly slice the red onions and throw them into a pot with the spices and oil. Cook over low heat, stirring occasionally, so the red onions and spices combine and cook evenly. When the red onions begin to sweat, add in a splash of water to avoid them sticking to the bottom of the pan. Once the red onions have cooked through, add in the sugar and golden raisins. Be sure to continuously stir the tfaya at this point to prevent it from sticking to the bottom of the pan. Once the red onions have caramelised, remove from the heat and set aside until you are ready to use the tfaya to top the couscous.

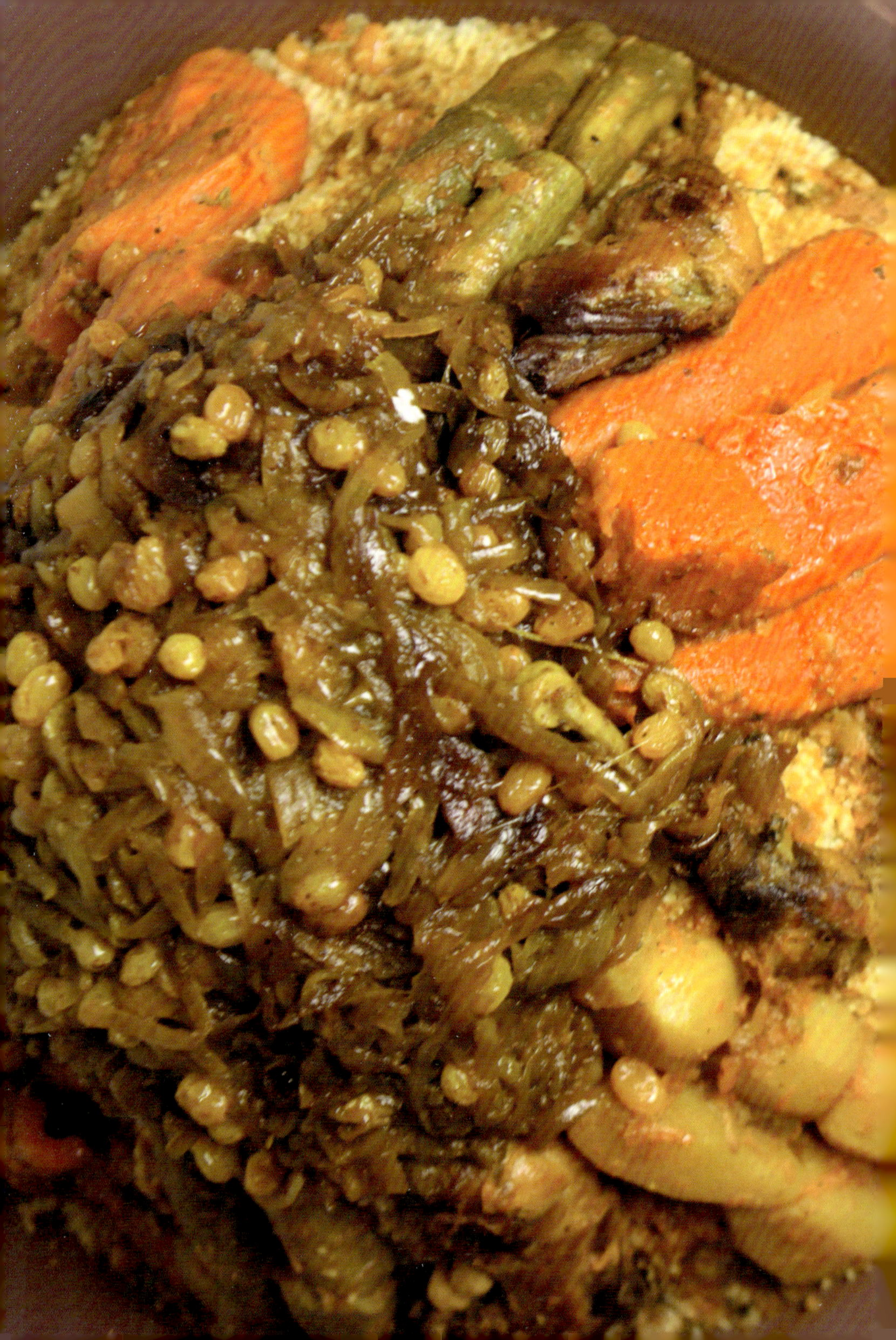

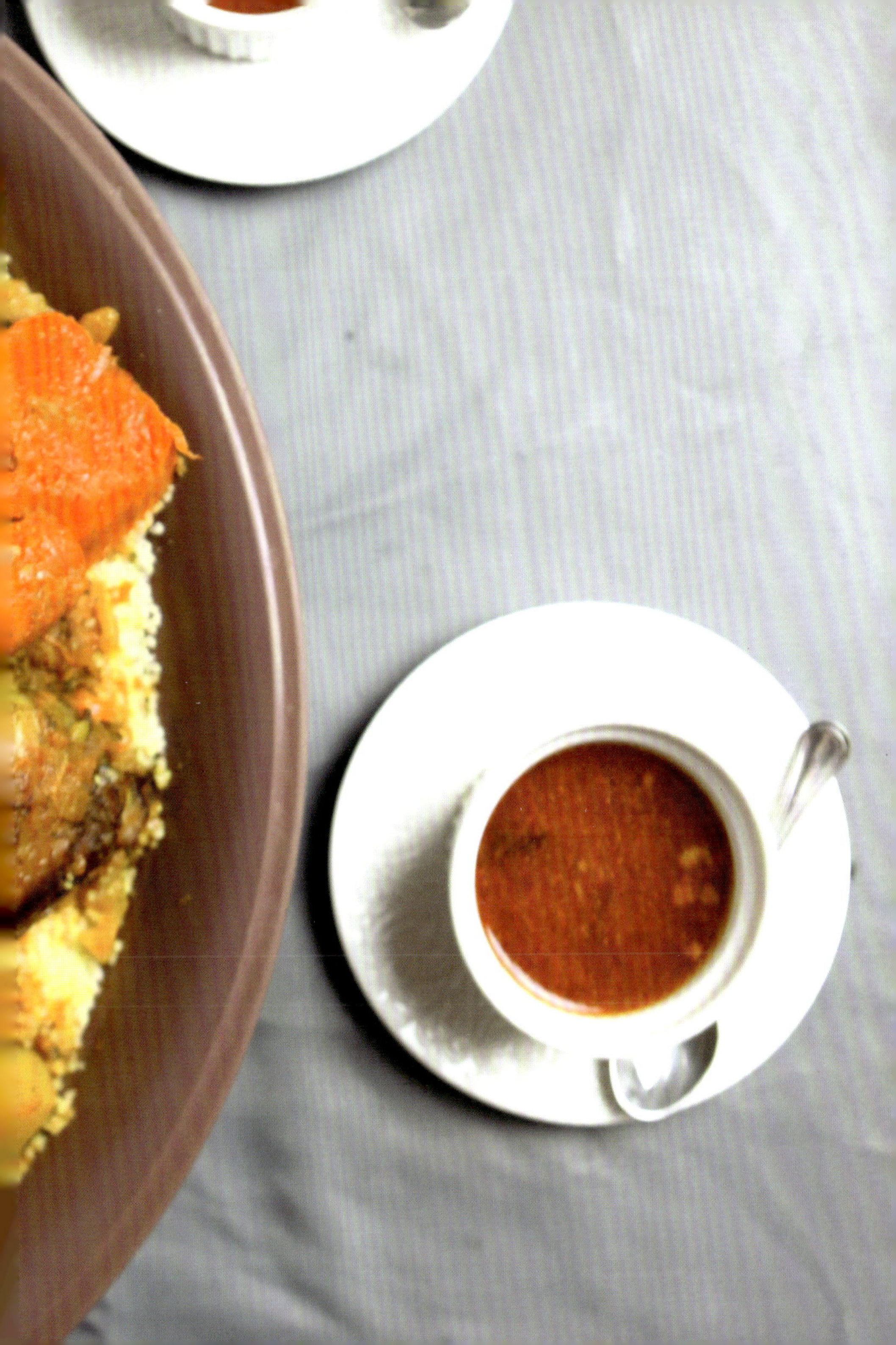

COUSCOUS WITH SEVEN VEGETABLES

Serves 6-8

Ingredients

½ kilo couscous

1 kilo mixed vegetables: tomato, aubergine, carrot, turnip, cabbage, pumpkin, potato, courgette

1 large red onion

1 small bunch fresh parsley and coriander

2 tablespoons olive oil

1 tablespoon of smen (or ghee, or any other clarified butter)

1 ½ teaspoons turmeric

1 teaspoon ground ginger

1 teaspoon paprika

1 teaspoon pepper

½ teaspoon ground saffron

Salt, to taste

Method

Thinly slice the red onion and dice the tomato. Then add to the bottom of a couscoussier (or a double boiler with holes on the bottom). Tie a string around the small bunch of parsley and coriander and throw that in along with the olive oil, spices, and salt and pepper to taste. Cook over medium high heat while you peel, trim, and halve the carrots and turnips and quarter the cabbage. Throw these all into the couscoussier followed by 1 ½ litres of water. Cover with the top part of the couscoussier.

Meanwhile, add the couscous to a large flat round bowl and splash in about 235 millilitres of cold water. Pour the water onto your hand over the couscous so that it splashes all around. Place into the top part of the couscoussier and cook until it starts steaming. Then, remove from the couscoussier and place back into the flat round bowl. Grab another 235 millilitres of cold water and splash over the couscous with your hands. Let the couscous cool down a bit before adding in 3 glugs of olive oil. Rub the couscous together with your hands until well-combined and then return to the top part of the couscoussier. Check on the vegetables and add another ½ litre or so of water if necessary. Once the couscous starts steaming again, remove it and splash in another 235 millilitres of water and 1 teaspoon salt. Rub altogether with your hands until combined. Replace the couscous and cook until steaming. Return to the large bowl and add in the smen and a final 300 millilitres water. Replace to the top of the couscoussier and let it cook until it starts steaming once again.

Plate the finished couscous in a large round bowl and top with the cooked vegetables and tfaya (see recipe on page 63). Serve the delicious sauce the vegetables were cooking in alongside the couscous.

Notes:

- Don't be pressured to follow the recipe, you are encouraged to make couscous with whatever vegetables you have in the fridge.

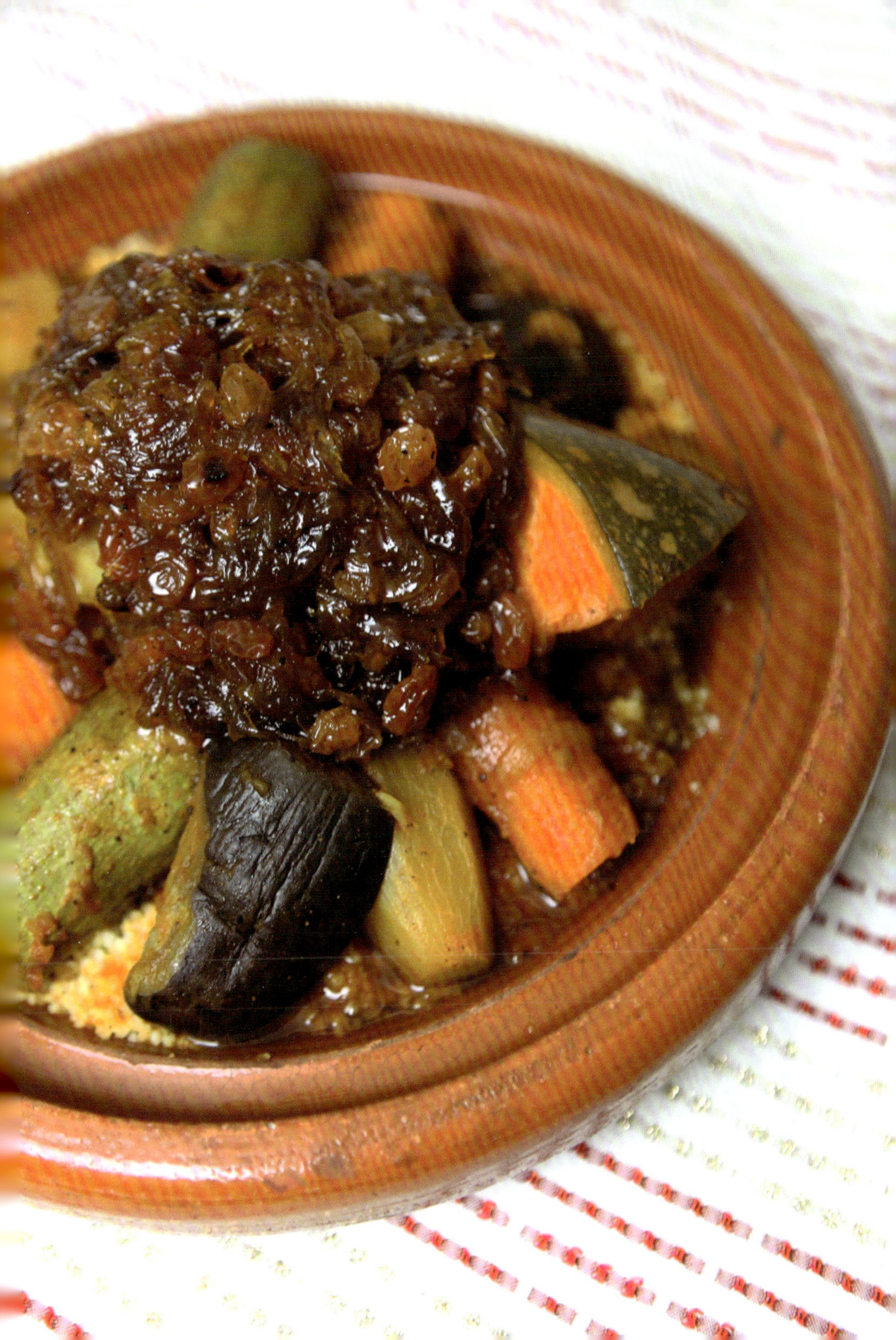

CHICKEN TAGINE WITH OLIVES & PRESERVED LEMON

Serves 2

Ingredients

- 1 kilo chicken, on the bone
- 1 teaspoon white vinegar
- Juice of ½ a lemon
- 2 tablespoons olive oil
- 1 ½ teaspoons salt
- 1 teaspoon ground ginger
- 1 teaspoon turmeric
- 1 teaspoon cumin
- ½ teaspoon pepper
- 3 cloves garlic, minced
- 2 red onions
- ¼ of a preserved lemon
- A large handful of chopped fresh parsley and coriander
- A small handful of green olives

Method

De-skin and trim the chicken before adding to a bowl with the white vinegar, lemon juice, and 1 teaspoon of salt. Mix to cover the chicken and then rinse under running water. Set aside.

Slice one of the red onions and layer it on the bottom of the tagine. Add the chicken, bone-side down. Top with the spices, minced garlic, a generous sprinkling of parsley and coriander, and a few slices of preserved lemon. Cook for 15 minutes, then flip and flip again so the spices and chicken get mixed altogether but the bone side is still down. Don't worry about uneven cooking, the tagine will ensure that the chicken gets cooked through. Add 250 millilitres of water, another generous sprinkling of the chopped fresh parsley and coriander, and another slice of preserved lemon for good measure. Cover and cook over medium high heat for 1 hour. Check halfway through cooking and add another 125 millilitres or so of water if the rest has cooked off. Top with green olives and serve warm with khobz.

Notes:

- This is often referred to as the Moroccan National Dish.

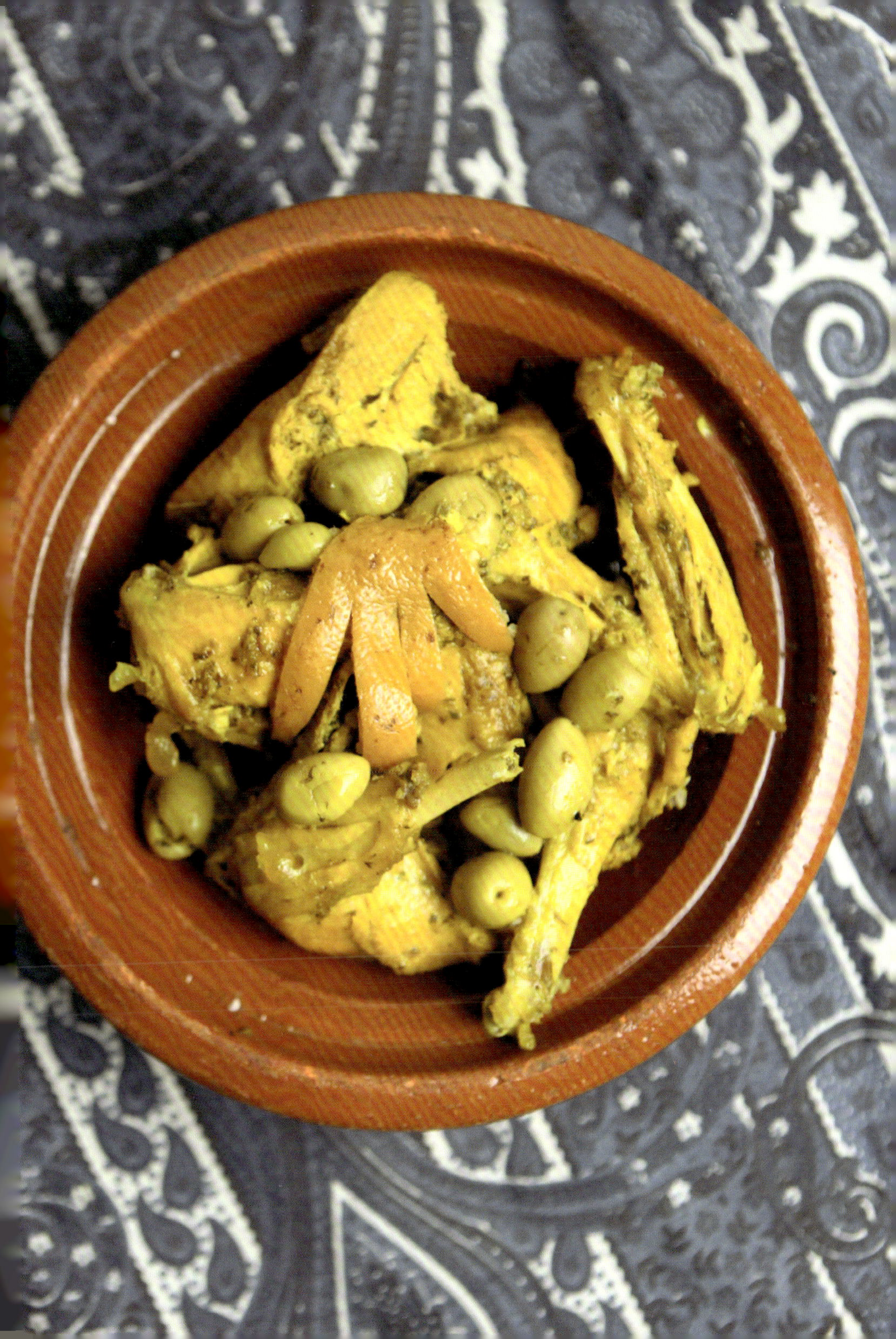

LAMB & VEGETABLE TAGINE

Serves 2

Ingredients

500 grams lamb
2 red onions
1 tomato
2 tablespoons sunflower oil
½ a tablespoon ground black pepper
½ a tablespoon ground ginger
¼ a teaspoon ground saffron
Salt, to taste
About a tablespoon each cinnamon and sugar to sprinkle on top

Method

Slice one of the red onions and lay flat on the bottom of a medium-sized tagine. Dice the lamb into 2 centimetre cubes and throw that in too. Sprinkle with the spices, a pinch of salt, and pour over the sunflower oil. Cover and cook over medium heat for 20 minutes. Turn the meat occasionally to brown on all sides. Pour in 2 cups of water and cover again. Let the tagine cook for half an hour while you thinly slice the remaining red onion and the tomato. Uncover the tagine and arrange the sliced red onion and tomato on top of the meat in a circular pattern. Then top with a generous sprinkling of salt, cinnamon, and sugar. Cook for another 20 minutes and serve with khobz.

Notes:

· Try this recipe out with beef.

· The addition of cinnamon and sugar with the meat, red onions, and tomato makes this a "Makfoul" tagine.

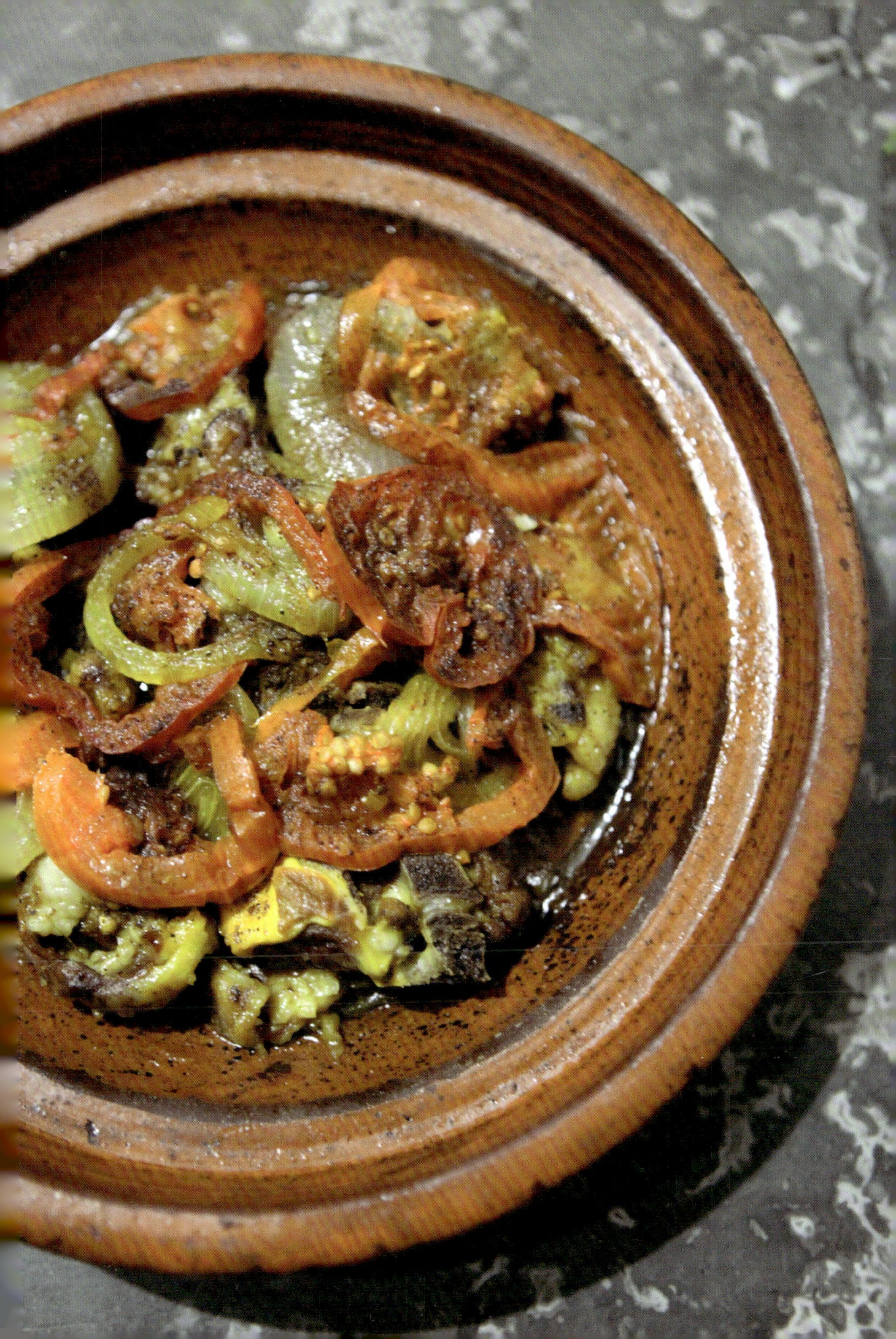

BEEF TAGINE WITH PRUNES & ALMONDS

Serves 4

Ingredients

1 kilo beef, trimmed and cut into thick strips

1 medium red onion

4 tablespoons olive oil

A little over a teaspoon each ground ginger, turmeric, and ras al hanout

Salt and pepper, to taste

A handful of raw almonds

6 boiled prunes, plus about 75 millilitres of their syrup

Method

Slice the red onion and arrange on the bottom of a medium sized tagine. Add the meat and sprinkle with the spices and olive oil. Cook over medium high heat for 10 minutes. Then, add enough water to cover the beef a quarter of the way up and put on the lid. Reduce the heat to medium low and cook for another hour. Check on the tagine halfway through cooking and add a bit more water if it is looking dry. Pour in about 3 tablespoons of boiled prune syrup at this point as well.

Meanwhile, blanch the almonds and fry them until golden brown, about 3-5 minutes. Then drain out any excess oil and set aside.

Once the meat is done, remove the tagine from the heat and sprinkle with toasted almonds. Garnish with the prunes, and then top each one with a sprinkling of sesame seeds. Serve warm with khobz.

BOILED PRUNES

Ingredients

2 handfuls dried prunes

3 teaspoons sugar

A generous sprinkling of cinnamon, a few cinnamon sticks, or both

Method

Toss the prunes into a pan and cover completely with water. Cook over high heat until half of the water has boiled off, about 10-15 minutes. Then, add sugar and cinnamon and continue to boil for another 10 minutes until most of the water has boiled off and you're left with soft, plumped prunes in a sugary syrup. These are incredibly versatile, and can be added to anything from tagine to an ice cream sundae.

Notes:

· This recipe works equally well with dried apricots or figs.

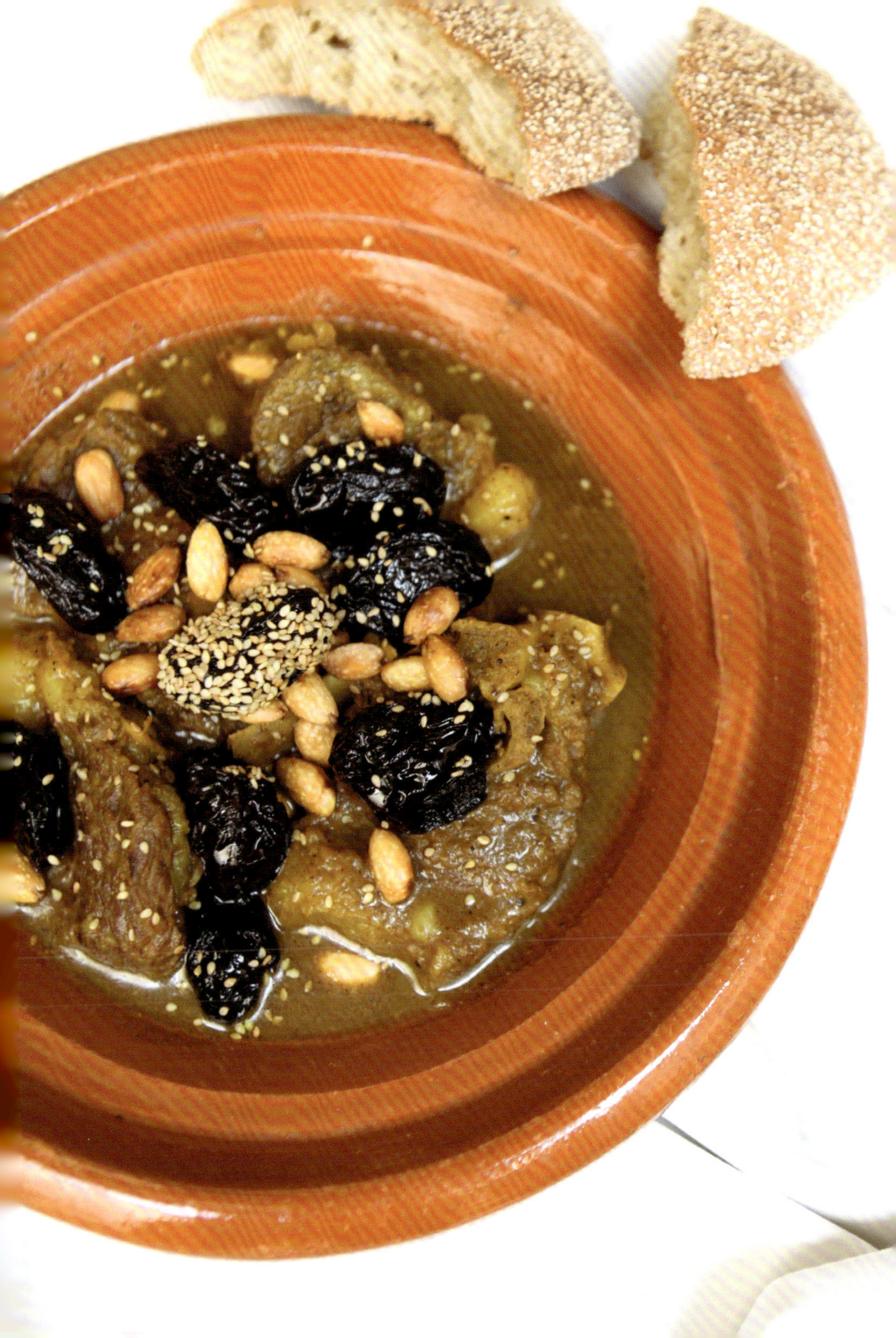

FISH TAGINE

Serves 2

Ingredients

500 grams of any firm white fish, we use Monkfish here
2 limes
2 tomatoes
A handful of chopped fresh parsley and coriander
3 large garlic cloves
Olive oil
1 teaspoon ground ginger

1 teaspoon turmeric
1 teaspoon cumin
¾ teaspoon paprika
1 large red onion
1 large carrot
1 potato
1 green bell pepper
Salt and pepper, to taste

Method

Halve both limes, deseed, and squeeze the juice of 1½ of them into a large bowl with the fish. Set the other lime half aside, you'll be using it later. Halve one of the tomatoes and grate each half over the bowl. Discard the tomato skin that will naturally come off. Add in the spices, parsley, coriander, and a few glugs of olive oil. Finely grate the garlic cloves over the bowl, too. Mix to combine and set aside to marinate while you prepare your vegetables.

Peel the carrot and the potato, and slice along with the red onion. Then core the bell pepper and cut into thick round slices.

Once the fish has had at least 10 minutes to marinate, layer the sliced red onion, fish, and vegetables on top of one another in a medium-sized tagine. Pour the rest of the marinade and another good glug of olive oil on top. Decorate the tagine with some lime slices (remember the one you saved?). Let cook for 20-25 minutes over medium heat and serve with khobz.

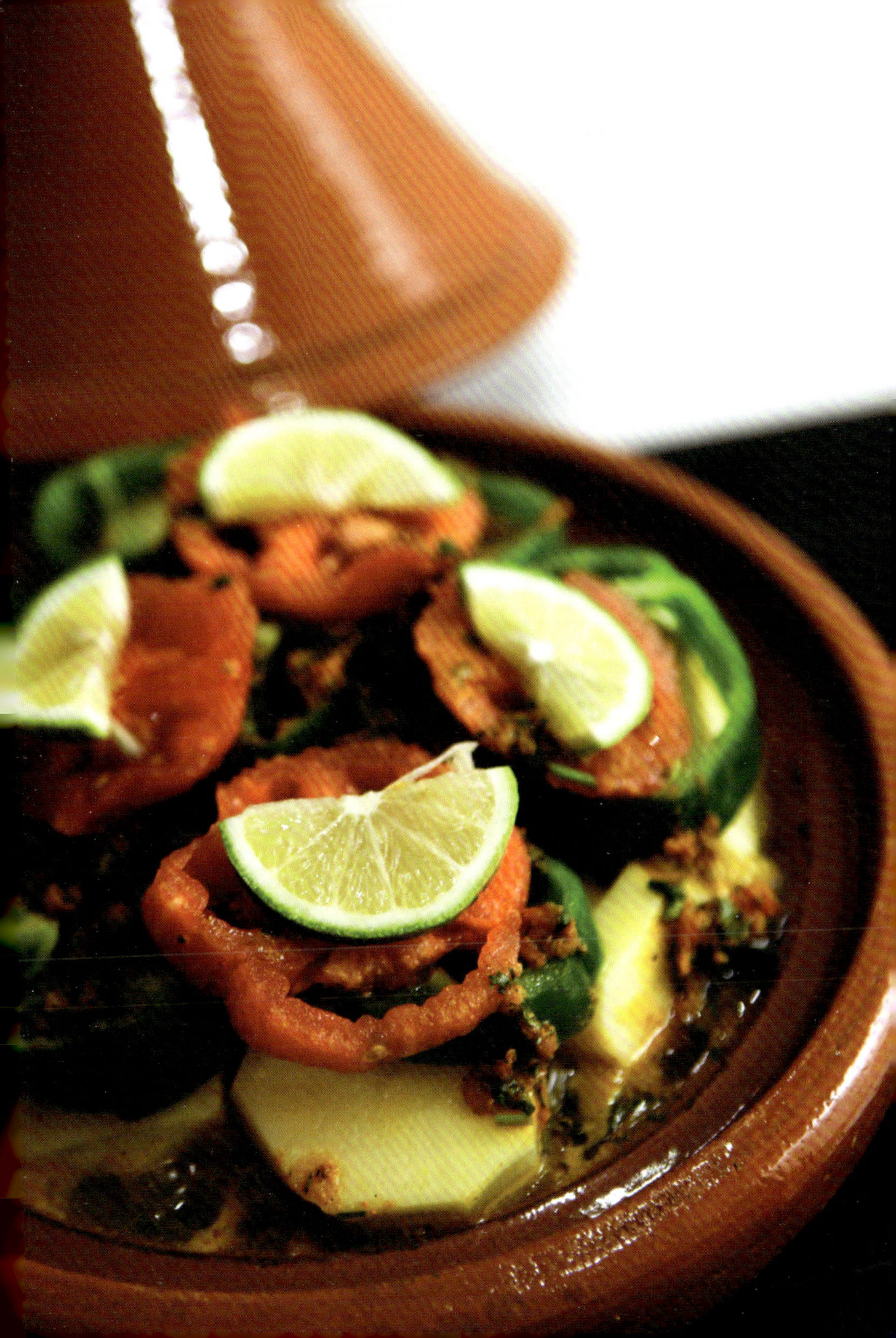

VEGETABLE TAGINE

Serves 2

Ingredients

1 large red onion
1 tomato
2 carrots
1 potato or turnip
1 courgette or squash
½ a bell pepper
3 glugs of olive oil
2 teaspoons ground ginger

2 teaspoons turmeric
1 teaspoon paprika
⅛ teaspoon ground saffron
3 garlic cloves
A small handful of chopped fresh parsley and coriander
Salt and pepper, to taste

Method

Slice the red onion, tomato, carrots, bell pepper, and peeled potato/turnip. Quarter the courgette/squash. Arrange the red onion on the bottom of a medium-sized tagine, and top with the rest of the vegetables. Then, grab a glass and pour in 125 millilitres of water. Mince the garlic and add it to the water with the spices, parsley, coriander, and a few glugs of olive oil. Give it a good stir, then pour atop the tagine. Cover and cook over medium-high heat for about an hour, or until the vegetables are cooked through. Garnish with a slice of lime and serve warm with khobz.

Notes:

- You can get creative here and arrange the vegetables in a design if you'd like, although we recommend you put the red onions on the bottom-most layer of the tagine so they have the opportunity to caramelise.

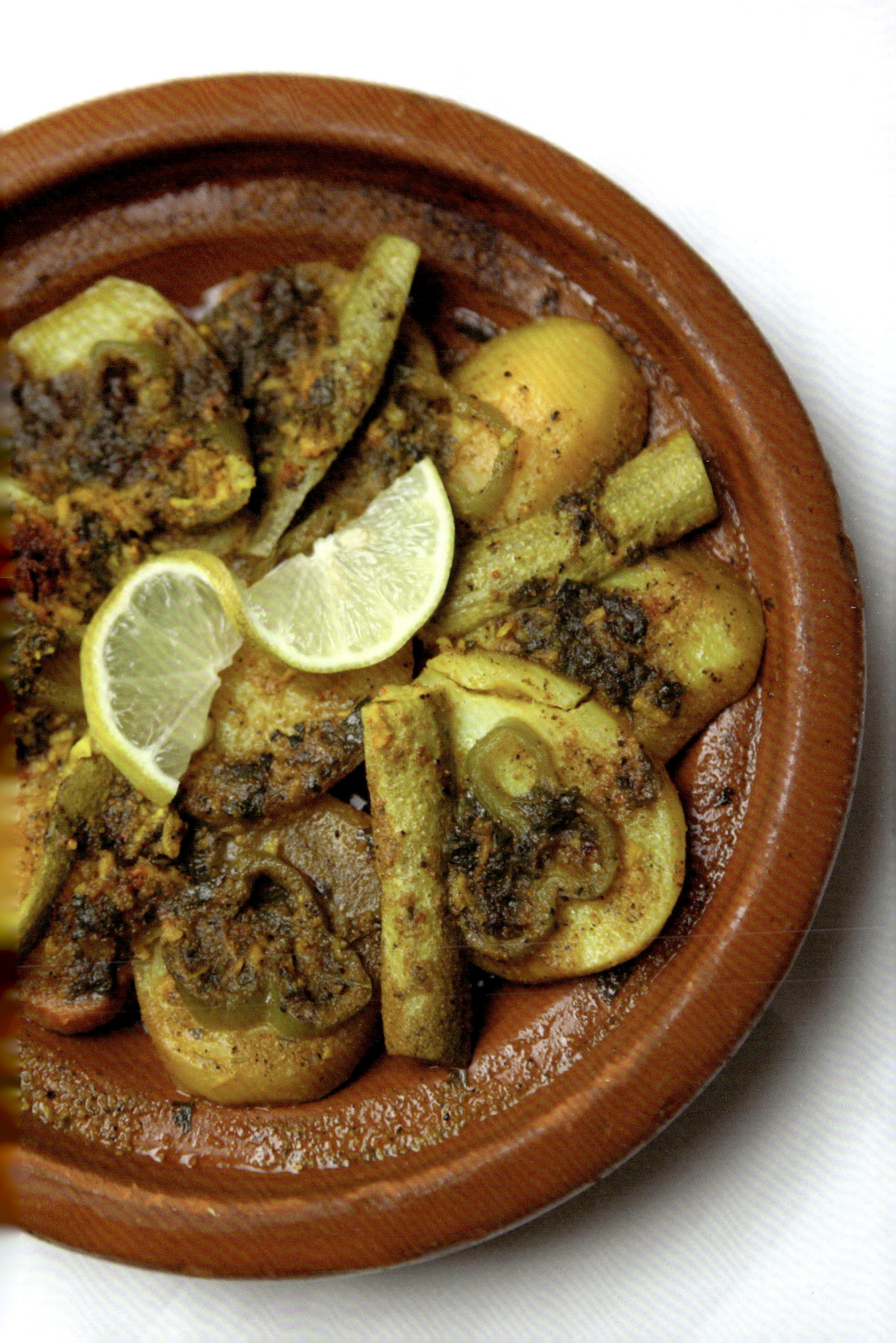

TANGIA

Serves 2

Ingredients

500 grams of lamb, cubed
½ a preserved lemon
7 cloves of garlic, peeled and halved
1 tablespoon salted smen
1 teaspoon ground ginger
1 teaspoon cumin
1 teaspoon pepper
¼ teaspoon ground saffron
60 millilitres olive oil

Method

Add all ingredients to a tangia pot with 600 millilitres of water and cover the top with a sheet of wax paper, using a string to seal it shut. Shake to combine and carry the tangia down the street to the farnatchi (the fire pit that heats the local hammam). If Si Mohammed isn't there, it's ok to leave it with his son. Spend your afternoon wandering the streets of the Medina and come back around 6 hours later. After paying a few dirhams, carry the tangia home, transfer to a serving dish, and eat immediately with khobz.

Notes:

- If you don't have access to a tangia pot, you can cook this dish in a cast-iron or terra cotta casserole dish. Simply toss in all of the ingredients, give it a good stir, and cook in a conventional oven at 100° C (212° F) for 6 hours. Remove from heat, place in a serving dish, and dig in.
- Ask your butcher not to trim the fat from your lamb. For best results, ask them to weigh out 500 grams of lamb with about 5-10% fat and 10% bone (bone cut into rings roughly 2-3 centimetres thick). The excess fat and bone marrow will melt into the dish and add flavour. Bones can be removed before serving or discarded when eating.
- Tangia is a dish that is traditional to Marrakech, cooked in a distinctive pot that shares the same name. The tangia is loaded up and taken to the local farnatchi where it is slow-cooked—not in the fire itself, but in the ashes which are stored in long troughs next to it. The management of the ashes is a treasured skill in and of itself, as they are routinely changed to assure even cooking of the tangias they hold. After roasting for 6 hours, locals pick up the tangias and take them back home to enjoy.

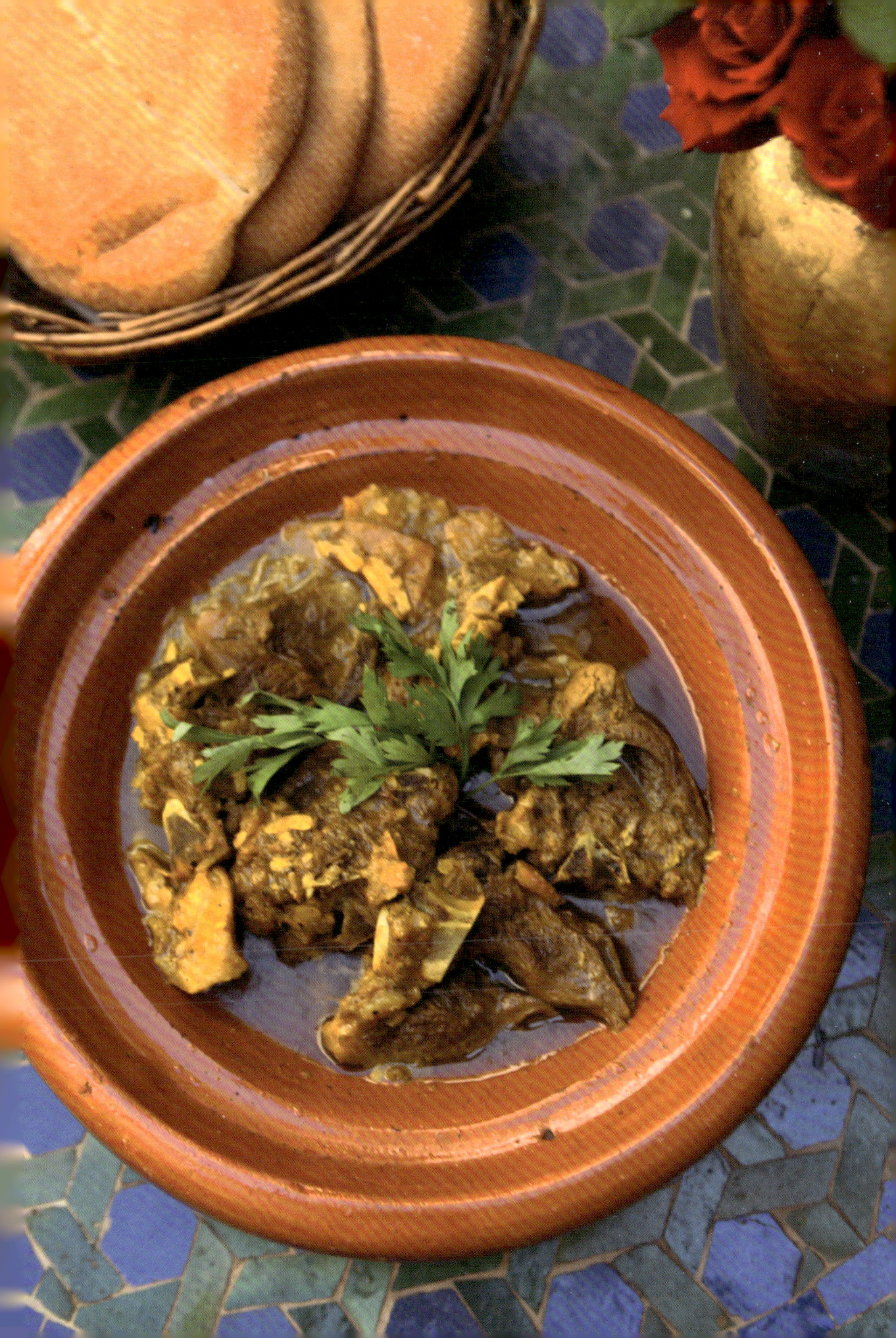

RIAD STAR

DESSERTS & TEAS

FRUIT BOWL

It is customary to offer fresh fruit at the end of a good meal in Marrakech. In our Riads we are proud to offer locally sourced seasonal fruit. The bowl pictured here is an Autumn Selection. When it comes to our fruit bowls, we don't reject misshapen fruits, as we believe it is the flavour that counts.

Bananas were first introduced to Morocco in the early 1940s. They thrive in the low frost-free area along the Atlantic coast north of Agadir. The most prolific variety is Dwarf Cavendish: these small sweet fruits are now a staple available all year round. Don't be put off by their modest exterior, they have an exquisite flavour, which can bring back childhood memories of how bananas used to taste.

Apples, pears and **plums** are grown about an hour from Marrakech in the fertile town of Asni in the foothills of the Atlas Mountains. The microclimate there is comparable to northern Europe, where deciduous trees flourish.

Pomegranate is a highly regarded fruit, as it is mentioned three times in the Quran. Our local suppliers are just outside of Marrakech in a small town called Chichaoua on the route to Essaouira where the season runs from late October until March. Eating them fresh can be a fun and messy business: first break the whole fruit open by hand or cut in half with a knife, then taste to determine the sweetness. Top with a splash of orange blossom or rose water to further enhance the flavour, or squeeze some lemon juice on top if it is too sweet. Scoop out the flesh and seeds with a spoon.

Peaches and nectarines from the High Atlas mountains are divine when perfectly ripe and juicy. The season begins earlier in Morocco than in Europe and it's not surprising that huge volumes are sent overseas in the early summer.

Cactus fruit (or prickly pears) are in season from July until September. Cactus fruit grows throughout Morocco where cactus hedges are common in rural areas. They should be opened cautiously with a sharp knife as the spines are fine and spiky. The inner fruit explodes with delightful flavours and is super healthy, packed with antioxidants and widely believed by locals to be good for an upset stomach.

Morocco has 300 days of sunshine and **oranges** are available throughout the year. It's during the winter months that their smaller cousins appear in the Marrakech Riad fruit bowl. **Mandarins**—squat in shape with lots of seeds—originated in the far-east. **Tangerines** are a mandarin hybrid which originated in the Northern Moroccan city of Tangier; they taste sweeter and stronger than an orange. Both are easy to peel and delicious.

Purple and green **grapes** come to us from Doukkala which is on the route to Essaouira. **Raspberries** and **strawberries** come from a region called L'Araish in the north.

Succulent **watermelon** is available throughout the summer. It helps quench thirst and keep people hydrated during the hottest months of the year. They are grown all over the country, but the watermelon from the dessert region of Zagora is undoubtedly the best with a national—and increasingly international—reputation.

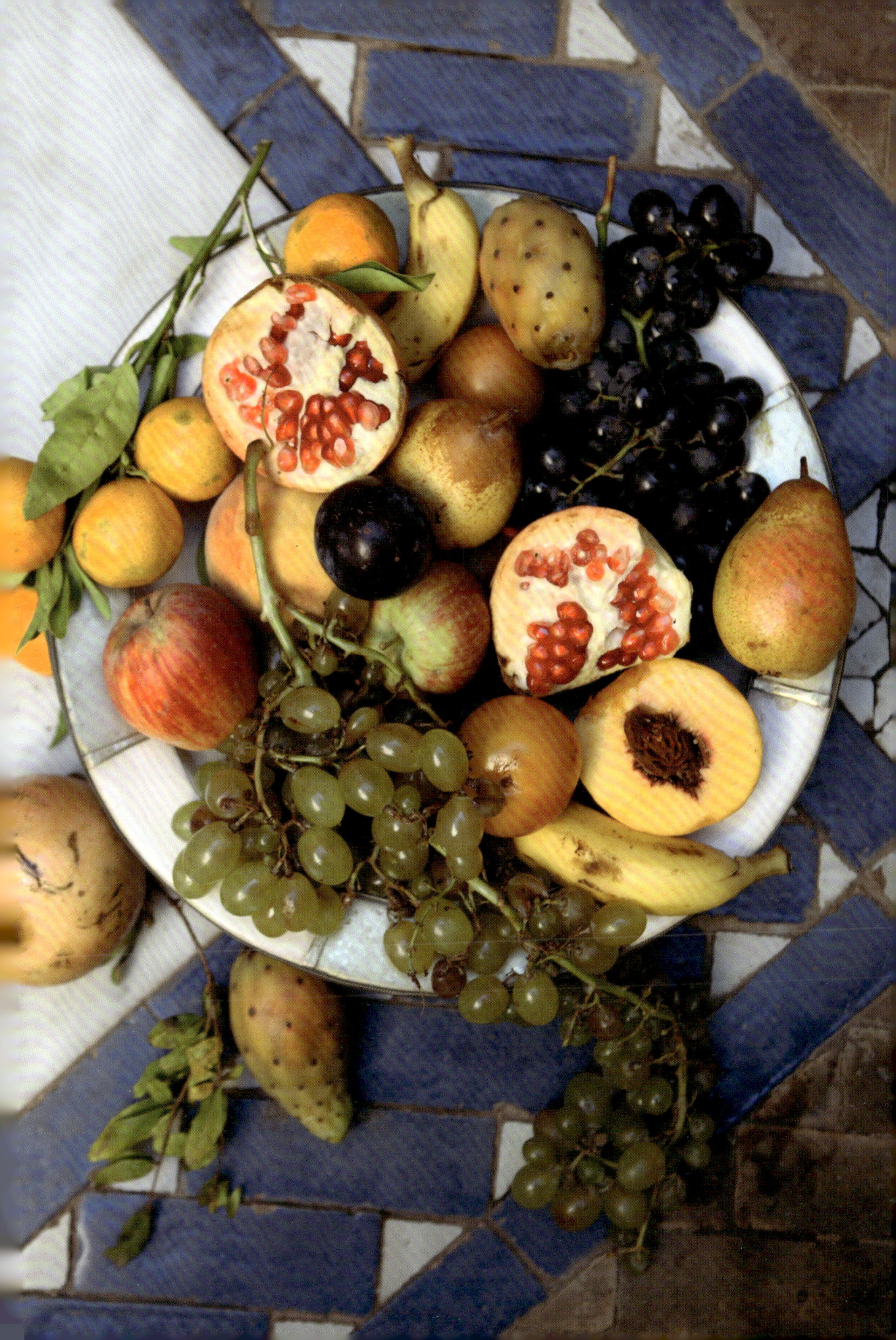

ORANGES WITH CINNAMON & SUGAR

Serves 2

Ingredients

2 oranges, preferably seedless navel oranges

A small handful of almonds

Sugar and cinnamon to sprinkle on top

Method

Using a sharp knife, cut off the top and bottom off of each orange. Then slice the rind away from top to bottom to remove as much as possible. Once all of the rind is gone, go back in with the knife to make sure the pith has been removed as well. Place the oranges on their sides and slice horizontally to your desired thickness, then lay out on a plate. Pulse the almonds in a grinder and sprinkle on top with the sugar and cinnamon. Serve.

Notes:

- In order to make the most of this dish, you need to understand your oranges. If they are in season, you will need very little sugar to sweeten them up. At other times of the year, you may need a lot more.

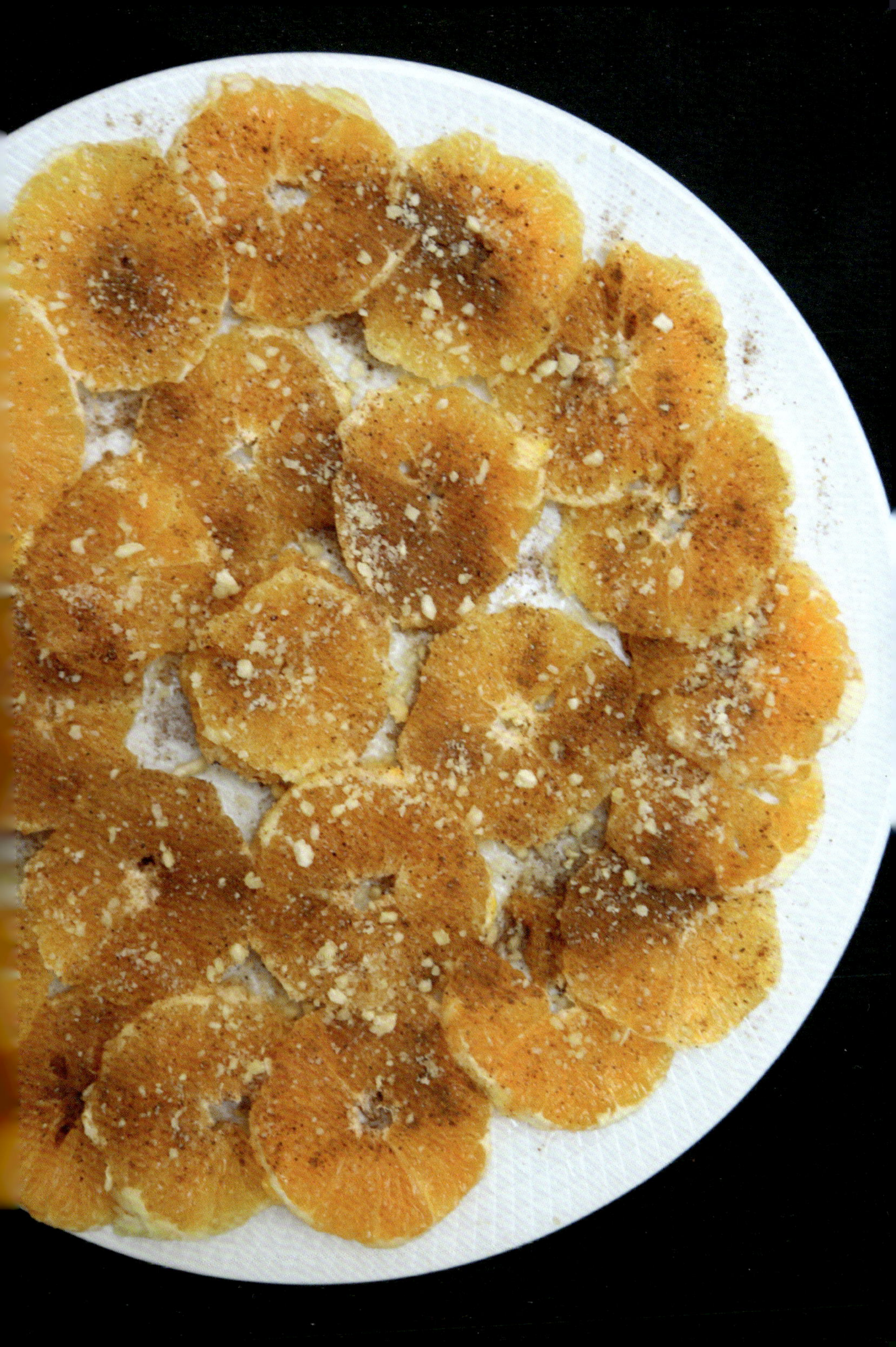

M'HENCHA

Serves 8

Ingredients

1 kilo raw almonds
½ a kilo filo pastry (circular sheets are preferred)
250 grams sugar
250 grams butter
150 grams powdered sugar

A few drops of orange flower essence
1 teaspoon cinnamon
⅛ teaspoon gum Arabic
Just a pinch of nutmeg
1 egg
Vegetable oil, for frying

Method

Blanch the almonds and fry in vegetable oil until golden brown. Set on a paper towel to drain out any excess oil. Set aside a handful of fried almonds in a small bowl before finely grinding the rest of them in batches with 1 teaspoon of sugar. Add another teaspoon of sugar with each small batch of almonds that you grind. Meanwhile, melt the butter and slowly pour it into the bowl with the sugared almonds and the rest of the ingredients (besides the egg). You only need to add enough butter to combine the mixture, and may not end up using the full amount stated above.

Cut all of the filo pastry in half so you end up with 2 half circles of layered dough. Lay an individual semi-circular sheet flat on a long counter. Lay another sheet on top so it covers half of the first one. You will end up with a long line of pastry sheets. Drop spoonfuls of the almond filling onto the straight edge of the pastry sheet, all the way down, and then begin slowly rolling it all up into a large cylinder. Then, roll the cylinder around itself so it forms a spiral. Beat the egg in a small bowl and brush the top of the m'hencha with the egg wash. Sprinkle any leftover butter on top of the m'hencha.

Bake in a 180° C (350° F) oven for 10-15 minutes or until the pastry is golden brown. Once finished, drizzle with mountain honey and sprinkle with cinnamon and the extra fried almonds.

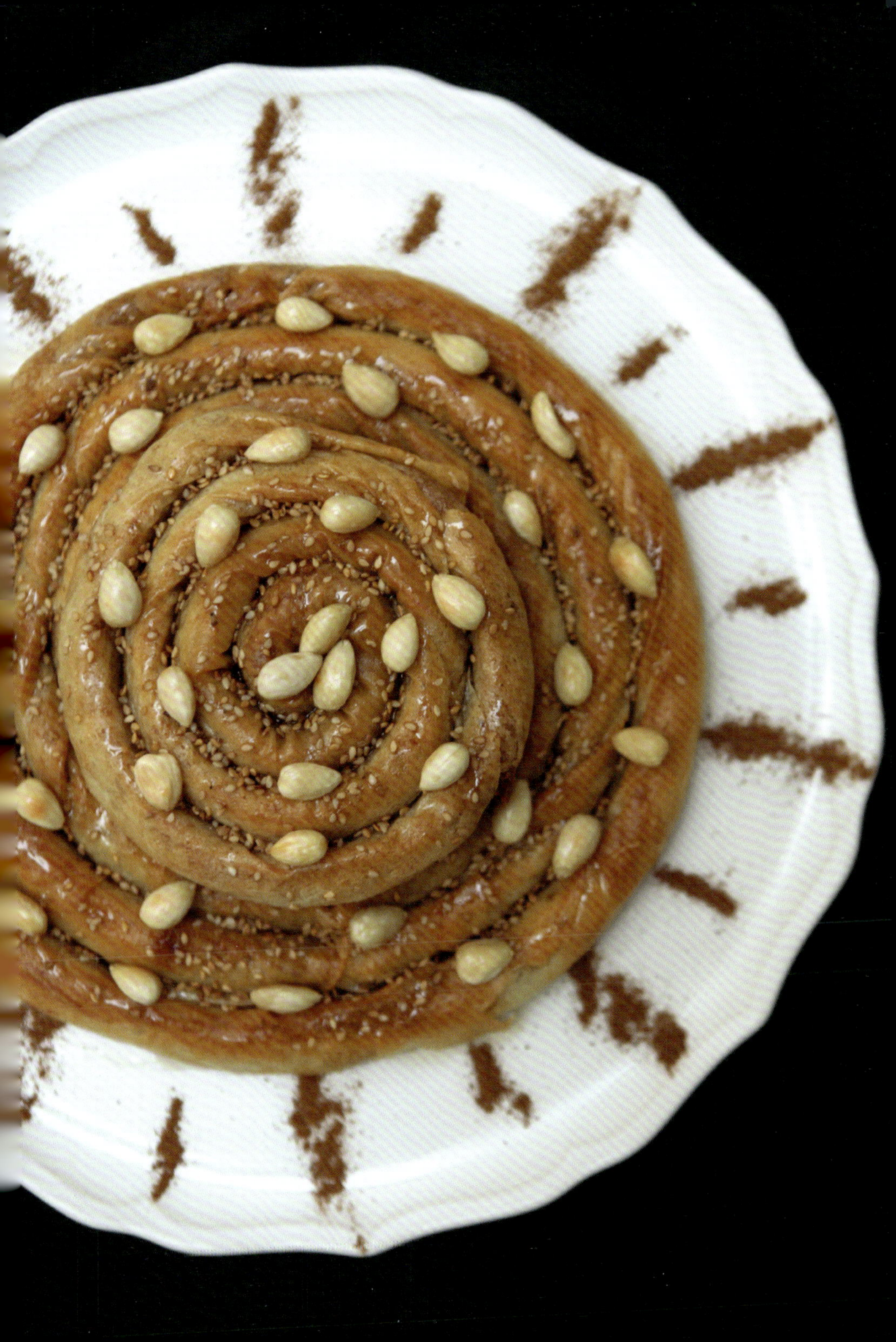

KRACHEL

Makes 15 rolls

Ingredients

1 kilo flour

1 cup sugar

115 grams of butter, softened

½ a cup of sunflower oil

300 millilitres milk

2 tablespoons orange flower water

2 teaspoons yeast

2 teaspoons of star anise seeds

1 teaspoon baking powder

1 teaspoon vanilla sugar (or substitute in a few drops of vanilla extract)

1 tablespoon sesame seeds, for topping

1 egg

Method

In a small bowl, dissolve the yeast in 3 tablespoons of warm (not hot) water. Meanwhile, add the flour to a large flat bowl and make a well in the center. Add the sugar, oil, butter, anise seeds, baking powder, vanilla sugar, orange flower water, and the activated yeast. Knead all together and then slowly add in the milk. The resulting dough should be very sticky. Add some more water or flour to get it to just come together.

Cover with cling wrap and let rise for 30 minutes. Knead once more and then cover with cling wrap again and let rise for another 30 minutes.

Shape small handfuls of dough into round balls and set on an oiled baking sheet to rest. Preheat the oven to 200° C (390° F) and flatten the balls lightly with your fingertips. Beat the egg in a small bowl and brush the rolls with egg wash, then sprinkle with sesame seeds. Bake for 15-20 minutes or until golden brown.

Notes:

· Serve these delicious little breads for breakfast or dessert.

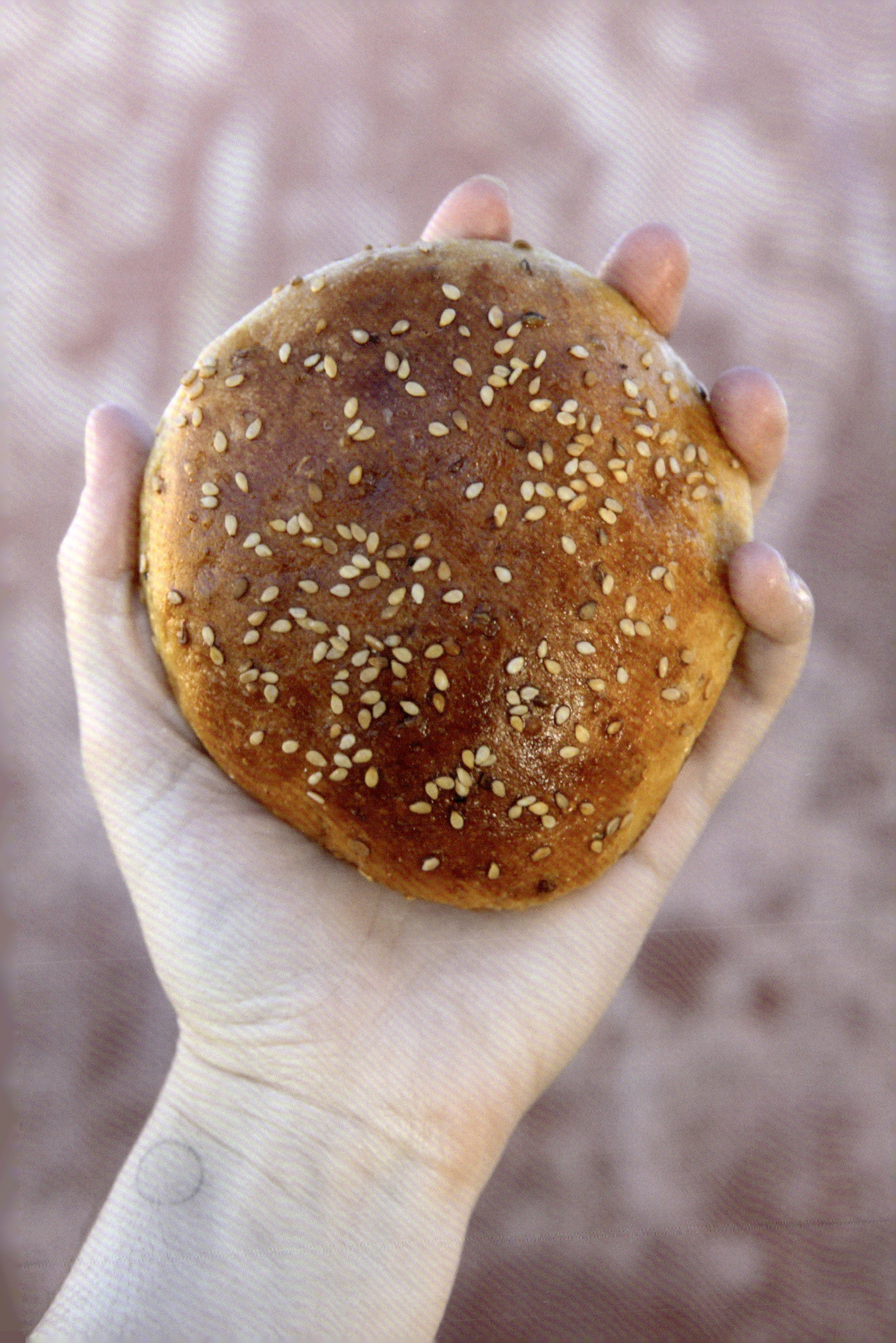

AMLOU

Serves 2

Ingredients

100 grams raw almonds

50 millilitres culinary argan oil

50 millilitres mountain honey (or the best honey you can get)

Sunflower oil, for frying

Method

Blanch the almonds and then fry in sunflower oil until golden. Place on a paper towel to cool completely and give them a rough chop before grinding in a high-powered food processor with the honey and argan oil. It's as simple as that!

Notes:

- Swap out almonds for any other nut for different flavour. Add more or less honey to taste, or a pinch of salt or cinnamon or both. Adjust the oil and honey measurements for a thicker or thinner amlou; Moroccans prefer a thinner, runny amlou that is easily pourable.
- This delicious nut butter is eaten for breakfast with matloa, baghrir, msemmen, etc. Use like any other nut butter (in sandwiches, smoothies, or with cut fruit). For a Brazilian/Moroccan fusion treat, trying topping an acai bowl with amlou.

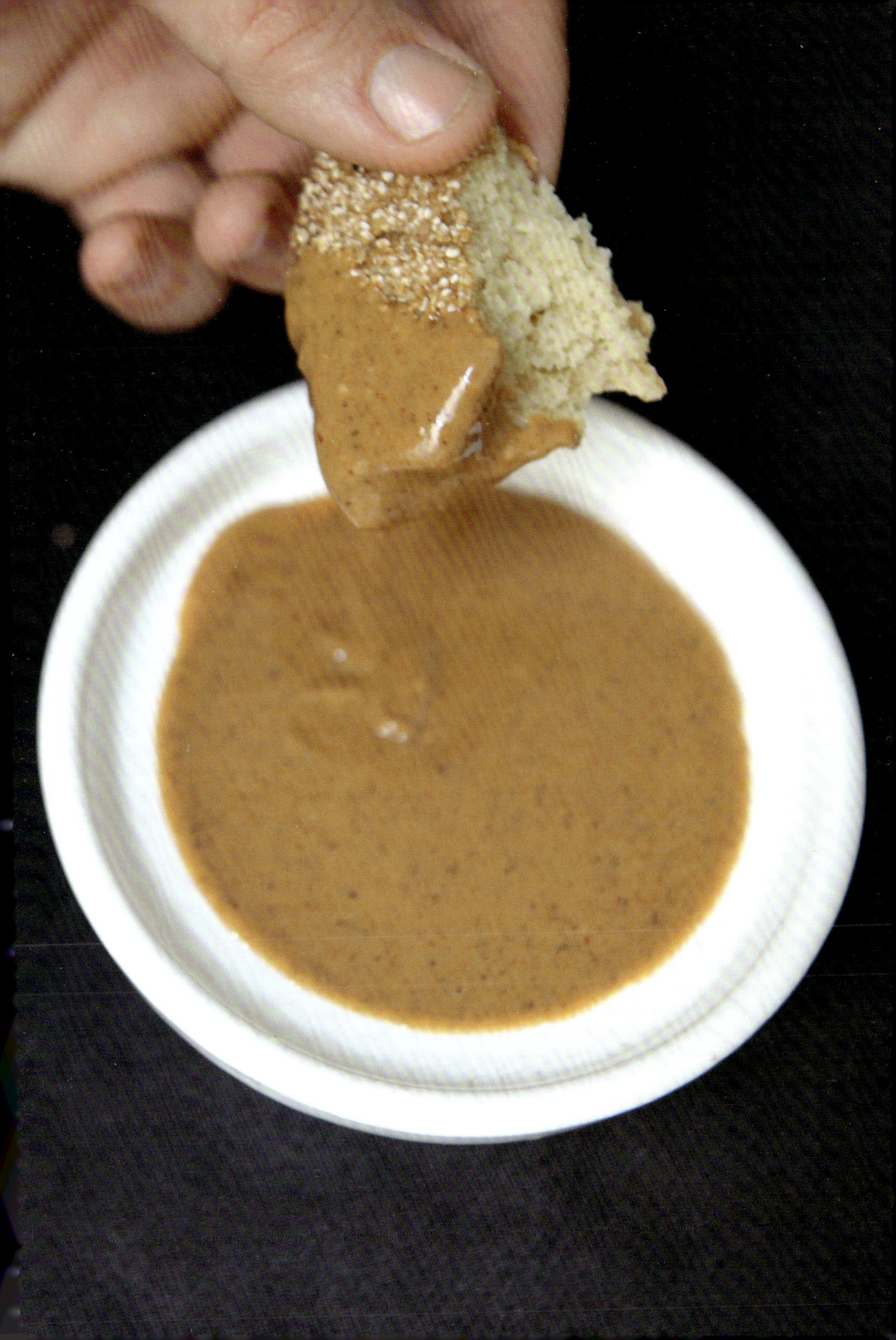

COCONUT COOKIES

Makes about 50 small cookies

Ingredients

For the dough:

235 millilitres vegetable oil

200 grams white sugar

7 grams vanilla sugar (or use a few drops of vanilla extract)

7 grams of baking powder

3 eggs

The zest of one lime

About 400 grams flour

To top:

About 300 grams apricot jam

About 200 grams finely shredded coconut

Method

Toss the first 6 ingredients into a steep-rimmed bowl and mix together with your hands until it all comes together into a dough. Gradually add the flour and continue to mix until the resulting dough is just slightly squishy. You know it's ready when you can easily pull a little piece off and roll it into a ball between your hands without it sticking.

Cover with cling wrap and let sit for 5 minutes. Then, pull off grape-sized pieces of dough and roll into balls. Place on a baking sheet and bake in a preheated 180° C (350° F) oven for 20-30 minutes, or until golden brown.

Then, using your fingertips, brush with apricot jam and roll in shredded coconut. Serve with mint tea.

Notes:

· Try these with any other jam, too! Fig jam is one of our favourites.

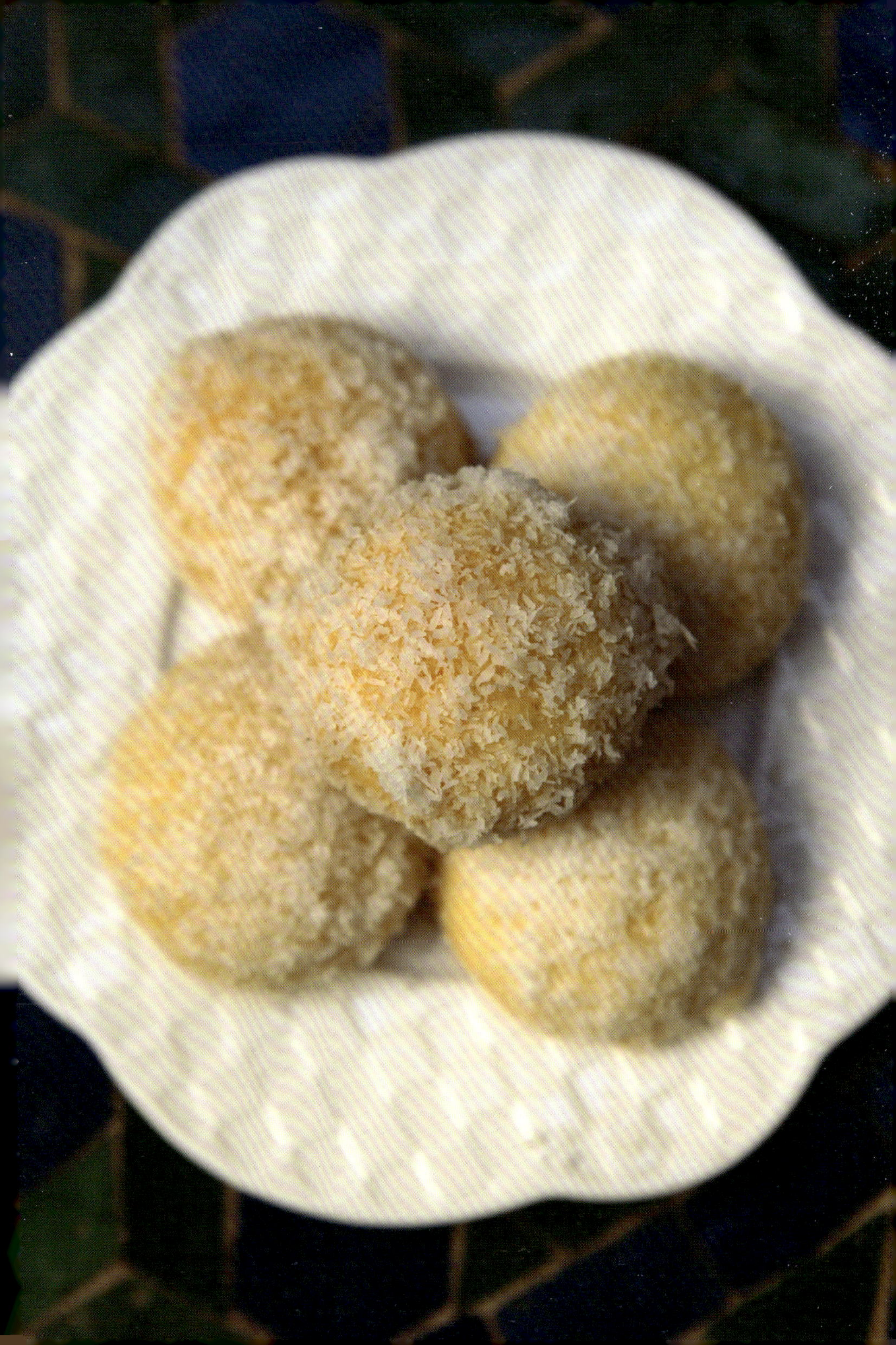

MOROCCAN MINT TEA

The first glass is as gentle as life; the second is as strong as love; the third is as bitter as death.

ARABIC PROVERB

Ingredients

Dried gunpowder green tea leaves
Fresh mint and herbs, ideally 7 varieties
Sugar (we use brown sugar cubes)

Method

Toss a generous spoonful of dried gunpowder green tea leaves into a large metal teapot. Then, rinse off fresh mint leaves along with the herbs of your choice, and stuff as much as you can into the teapot. Add boiling water. Then, light a gas burner and adjust to high heat. Set the tea pot directly over the flame. Once the tea begins bubbling excessively, remove from heat. Lift the tea pot, pour the tea into a small glass teacup from as high as you can, and then return the tea back to the teapot. This is called "rinsing" or "cleaning" the mint tea, and is done anywhere from 1 to 6 times before pouring a cup of tea. When the tea is a beautiful deep yellow-green colour, pour a glass and add as much sugar as you'd like. Serve warm with coconut cookies (see recipe on page 92).

Notes:

- There are over 600 varieties of mint in the world! To learn more about the most popular varieties used in Morocco, turn to page 15.
- We serve our tea with sugar on the side, but most Moroccans add sugar directly to the teapot before serving.
- It is important to pour the tea from very high above the cup because it helps to aerate and develop the tea's flavour.
- Moroccans believe that the more bubbles you have in your tea, the better.
- You'll find that as you drink a pot of tea the flavour will change from cup to cup as the leaves continue steeping in the pot.

"Marrakech is our passion, we look forward to sharing it with you."

BE OUR GUEST

Fourteen years ago, we began the painstaking renovation of Riad Cinnamon in the old town medina. Today, we are proud to offer five boutique hotels all within a short walk of the main square: Riad Papillon, Riad Cinnamon, Riad Dar Habiba, Riad Star, and Riad Spice. What really makes us special is our small team of dedicated staff who will be on hand to help, reassure and advise throughout your stay.

It's the little things that count: the loan of a local cell-phone; luxurious cotton sheets; orange blossom toiletries; a delicious breakfast served at the time of your choice and authentic cuisine prepared to your taste and dietary requirement. Every meal is shopped for and prepared to order.

SMARTPHONE APP

Our "Marrakech Riad Travel Guide" features an offline map of Marrakech complete with our recommendations in and around the Medina. Use the built-in GPS feature to determine your precise location. We have also added information on our favourite monuments, museums, shops, bars, restaurants, and foodie hotspots for you to use as a springboard for further exploration. The app is free to download for Apple and Android users, and works without internet connection. Happy exploring!

MOROCCAN COOKERY COURSE

Join us for a half-day course in one of our Riads and learn to cook these and other dishes first-hand. Visit the local vegetable and spice market to select ingredients before preparing two seasonal starters and one main dish, which is usually a tagine.

The course runs between 2pm and 6pm and at the end of the afternoon you will enjoy eating the food you have prepared with the other course participants. Non-residents are welcome.

FOODIE BREAK

We hope you have enjoyed reading the Marrakech Riad Cookbook, and have tried a few recipes. We invite you to our "Flavours of Marrakech" break which includes three nights staying with us at the Riad of your choice, airport transfers, a delicious evening meal on arrival, fantastic breakfasts with European options and local specialities, our Cooking Course, and a private half-day food heritage walking tour in the old town medina with a charismatic guide.

Mike & Lucie

www.marrakech-riad.com

MARRAKECH RIAD COOKBOOK

ACKNOWLEDGEMENTS

We would like to thank our guests for their support and are proud to acknowledge those partners and colleagues, too numerous to mention individually, who have contributed to our team at Marrakech Riad.

Particular thanks go to our translator Zouhair; our chefs Hanan, Meriem, Loubna, Yassmin, Bahija, Zahira, Amina, Sana, and Khalifa; and our guardians Abdou, Ali, Mohamed, Hussein, and Rachid.

Many thanks also to our recipe testers Abi, Charley & Denise, Colin & Claire, Pete, Michael, Ros, Maria, Diana & Andrew, Bianca, Claire, Siobhan & Neil, Julia, Wendy and Anne. And a big thank you to our proofreaders Edwin & Irene, Sarah, Brad, and Michael.

This book would not have been possible without the dedication and commitment of our super talented researcher Hannah Lansill who spent hundreds of hours in the kitchens of our Marrakech Riads mastering these recipes and their variants, as well as the local Darija dialect. Hannah also staged and took all of the mouth-watering food photographs.

RIAD STAR